SBAC

Talent
MAKERS

Daniel Chait and Jon Stross

Talent
MAKERS

How the best organizations win through
structured and inclusive hiring

WILEY

Published by John Wiley & Sons, Inc., Hoboken, New Jersey.
Published simultaneously in Canada.

For general information on our other products and services or for technical support, please contact
our Customer Care Department within the United States at (800) 762-2974, outside the United
States at (317) 572-3993 or fax (317) 572-4002.

Wiley publishes in a variety of print and electronic formats and by print-on-demand. Some material
included with standard print versions of this book may not be included in e-books or in
print-on-demand. If this book refers to media such as a CD or DVD that is not included in the
version you purchased, you may download this material at http://booksupport.wiley.com. For more
information about Wiley products, visit www.wiley.com.

Library of Congress Cataloging-in-Publication Data is Available:
ISBN 9781119785279 (Hardcover)
ISBN 9781119785293 (ePDF)
ISBN 9781119785286 (ePub)

COVER DESIGN: PAUL MCCARTHY
COVER IMAGE & AUTHOR PHOTOS: © GREENHOUSE SOFTWARE, INC.

SKY10026177_040821

This book is dedicated to everyone who has ever hired someone, or been hired.

Contents

Talent
MAKERS

1

The Problem and the Promise

The war for talent is over.
Talent won.

If you're the leader of an organization or a team, it's a pretty safe bet that time is precious to you. You want people to get to the point quickly. We'll do that for you right now. Here's this book in a nutshell:

- People know that hiring is important.
- They know that their "system" of hiring is broken.
- They don't know how to fix it.

This book is not for HR professionals, though they may benefit greatly from it. Instead, this is a book for you the leader of a team of any size. It will give you specific, actionable advice about how you can not only fix your hiring problems, but how you can turn hiring into an astonishing competitive advantage. You will improve your hiring quickly, substantially, and measurably. If you wish, you can do all of this *without* buying any software. The transformation will not be easy, but we will lay out for you a proven method to make it work.

There you have it. That's the book.

1

If you've reached a point where you have had enough with the pain and chaos of hiring and you want to get really good at it, then you've come to the right place.

The Sorry State of Hiring

We'll get much more detailed later, but let's take a quick, depressing tour of what hiring looks like in a great many organizations. We'll look at hiring from several different perspectives.

Candidates

You may have spent a lot of time thinking about your brand. You may even have detailed, expensive campaigns that focus on what you want to be known for in the mind of your target audience.

Then there's Glassdoor.

It has 50 million unique monthly visitors. It only takes a few clicks to see what employees right now are saying about your brand, and what candidates are saying about the interviewing and hiring process.

Within minutes of walking out of an interview, candidates will post reviews with explicit descriptions of how they were treated. Occasionally, those observations are good; much more often they sound like this:

- "I sat in an empty room for a half hour. I think they forgot about me."
- "The interviewer walked in and said, "Now, you're here for which job?"
- "I'm a woman and was being interviewed for a technical position. The interviewer sat down and goes, 'Maybe you'd be interested instead in the position we have in our design department?'"
- "I have a name that's not common in America. Throughout the interview they butchered my name and couldn't even settle on one *incorrect* pronunciation even after I corrected them."

Anyone can view Glassdoor ratings. But we at Greenhouse benefit from an additional, eye-opening vantage point by virtue of having more than 4,000 organizations as customers. We also live and breathe hiring, so we hear a lot about hiring practices at organizations of all sizes and stripes. Here are typical situations.

Interviewers

We regularly hear words to the effect of "Shortly before I'm supposed to interview someone, the recruiter will hand me a résumé and say, 'Spend an hour with this person. Tell me if she's any good.'"

Interviewers are often given no training or instruction on how to conduct a good interview. In addition, they may have no idea what other interviewers will ask or who they even are. As a result, candidates will have three people in a row say to them, "So, tell me about your last job." Untrained, clueless interviewers will also ask irrelevant or even downright illegal questions, like "Are you planning on getting pregnant?"

When there is no interviewing plan, it's common for interviewers to ask one-size-fits-all questions. They may spend time during the interview brainstorming what their next question will be when the candidate stops talking instead of focusing on what the candidate is saying at the moment.

And because there is no coordination between interviewers in terms of who asks what, gaps can occur where no one asked about important aspects of the job.

If there is no discipline around writing down one's impression right after interviewing a candidate, then soon all those sessions blur together:

"I thought Chantelle was good."

"Was she the one in the green sweater?"

"No, you're thinking of what's-her-name. ... "

Recruiters

Recruiters are extremely busy people, even in the best-run operations. They do heroic work, often with little or no credit. In most organizations, they struggle to keep up and are always putting out fires.

If the day of the week ends in a "y", then the pressure will be on to deliver candidates. Recruiters are often given extremely little information about the positions they're supposed to fill right away. At these organizations, recruiting is the recruiter's job—a largely administrative one with no recognition. For everyone else, it's a burden that takes away from their "real job."

A recruiter may identify ten candidates and send them to the hiring manager with a note: "Here's the latest. Tell me what you think. Are these the kind of candidates you're looking for?" They'll get back an email with this helpful, descriptive reply:

"No."

Recruiters may go to great lengths to piece together interviews for a sought-after candidate to fill a key role, only to have an interviewer show up late or not at all.

Sometimes the pressure on recruiters will result in their not taking the time to use the Applicant Tracking System (ATS) or other tools in the department: "Hey, do you want me to fill these openings, or do you want me to fill out forms?" Soon, this means the tools do not reflect reality and therefore, aren't useful, so why bother to update them? A classic downward spiral.

Hiring Managers

Hiring managers routinely feel as if they're in the dark and are frustrated. They're the ones who requested that a role be filled. They are on the line to fill that role in order to make their numbers, yet they have little meaningful data, no transparency as to what's going on, and no predictability. They often feel as if they're at the mercy of the recruiter and are forever asking, "Where are we? What's going on with this job?"

Just as recruiters under pressure will ignore the systems and tools, hiring managers under pressure will take matters into their own hands. A few years ago, we asked the head of equity derivatives trading at a very major firm how he hired. He said:

> How do I make a hire? Here's how it works. I need to hire a trader in Manhattan. I tell someone in HR, and someone in Cincinnati emails me a Word document with a job description. It's absolutely meaningless B.S. It has nothing to do with my business. It's a bunch of jargon. So I look at it, okay, whatever. And then they go away for

three months and tell me that they're recruiting for this role. And I hear nothing, I know nothing. Many weeks later, they still haven't made the hire or even sent along any candidates. So, I go take my buddy out for a beer. He's an equity derivatives trader at my old firm. He hooks me up with a couple of people he knows who are solid traders and I meet with them. I really like one. I then email HR and say, 'I got this person; here's their résumé. They're perfect for the job, so hire them.' HR puts the person in the system and they get hired."

It turned out that the formal hiring process at the firm added zero value and the managers were left on their own to figure out how to hire. The hiring of the new trader was not based on a rigorous, structured process that would have helped to minimize bias and deliver the best candidate.

Because hiring managers feel such pain around the process, they may hold onto underperforming employees much longer than they otherwise would: "Maybe I'll suffer with this person and make do; after all, who knows how long it will take to get that role filled again?"

The C-Suite

A venture capital (VC) firm put on a conference for CFOs and invited us to speak about the ROI of good hiring practices. These were some tough, numbers-driven folks. At the end of the presentation, one guy said, "Okay, okay, I accept your premise. I accept your framework for how to think about hiring and I think you're right. That *is* how we should think about it. But this is HR! If I give them that money, I won't get any of the results you're talking about."

That type of comment is indicative of a breakdown in communications between the recruiting and business sides of the organization. That leads to the downward spiral of lack of trust and lack of funding. The C-suite can be a place where maximum pressure to deliver results meets maximum distance from detailed information about the status of hiring:

- "We're trying to grow and it's not working."
- "We've spent a ton of money on systems and I can't get any decent reports."

- "We know that we have an issue with meeting our diversity, equity, and inclusion targets, yet all I hear are generalities about 'It's a top-of-funnel problem; there just aren't enough engineering applicants who are women.'"
- "We have as a goal to increase the number of people we promote from within, and we post all the positions. Why is it that we always have to look outside to get the key roles filled?"

Employees Who Refer Friends

Even poorly run organizations recognize the cost savings when employees successfully refer friends for jobs. As we'll talk about in Chapter 6 about finding the best talent, internal referrals are indeed a great thing.

When employees refer their friends, their personal brand or reputation is now at stake. If the hiring experience goes well, then friends stay friends. But too often it's a case where the employee hears about her friend's terrible experience—or never hears anything—and is embarrassed for herself and for the organization: "Oh my gosh, I'm so sorry. It's actually a good company, but that was an awful experience they put you through." That has a way of quickly drying up the referral channel.

What Hiring Looks Like at the Best Companies

You should know right up front that when we refer to "the best companies," we do not mean the companies that have the largest list of amenities like gourmet chefs, dog walkers, and dry-cleaning services. Those may be nice, but in some cases they can be poor investments, as we'll see in Chapter 3 when we discuss the ROI of hiring.

Instead, we're referring to the companies for whom hiring has become a huge competitive advantage. It's become woven into their culture so that people support each other to do the right things, and pressure each other when someone reverts to the old ways.

Speaking of the old ways, it's common for people to spend decades being employed in multiple organizations and for them never to see hiring done right. It's always been a mess wherever they worked, so they just kind of assume that "it is what it is" everywhere. Here is what great hiring looks like.

Candidates

When people come across your job posting, the first thing they'll notice is that it's not this dry-as-dust, bureaucratic-sounding document with specifications. It sounds more like an enticing advertisement than a job posting.

If they get an interview, they'll get a detailed document giving them all that information they would otherwise sweat about: where to park, what door to enter, what to wear, and what will happen.

The candidate will have recorded his or her name in advance, so everyone that day will know exactly how to pronounce it.

The interview experience will be friendly and crisp, with each interviewer meshing with the other interviewers, so relevant questions get asked once and all the bases get covered.

At the end of the interview, the candidate will know exactly what the next steps are, and when they'll happen.

When candidates are treated this way, it's not uncommon for them to leave positive Glassdoor reviews *even when they did not get the job*.

Perhaps most important of all is what happens when you're after the most-sought-after people to join your organization: You can bet that they're weighing multiple job offers and checking out Glassdoor. You can also bet that most of those other hiring experiences will suck.

Interviewers

As soon as you get scheduled for an interview, there's a link in the invite that says you're going to go interview Robbie MacGregor. You click on it and are taken to page with everything you need to conduct a great interview:

- The tasks that are expected of you
- The list of questions you will ask
- A link to any material we have on Robbie, like his résumé and supporting documents he sent in
- The scorecard that you must fill out right after the interview. It's got all the criteria that have been agreed upon as important for this particular job. It is by no means a one-size-fits-all scorecard.

When you meet with Robbie, you are relaxed and attentive because you're following a clear and effective system. After you meet with him, you make a point to fill out that scorecard promptly and completely because you don't want a repeat of that one day when you were called out by the rest of the team for wasting their time.

Recruiters

In the best companies, recruiters are still extraordinarily busy people. But it's a good busy, because they're treated as partners by the hiring managers. They know each other's roles, and there's a mutual respect between them.

Before any applicants are screened or interviewed, the recruiters will be brought up to speed about what this job involves, how it's different from last year's positions, what the key requirements are, and what phrases or lingo to use so that candidates know they're speaking with a person who actually knows something about the position.

Recruiters live in the department's tools, meaning that they use those tools and systems rather than create their own spreadsheets on the side. Better discipline around tools and systems results in more reliable data.

Hiring Managers

Hiring managers still have the stressful challenge of meeting deadlines and goals, but the big difference is they're not doing so in the dark. Systems are not only continually updated, but they work in concert with each other, and that brings a level of regular awareness about the current hiring trajectory in relation to goals.

When the time comes to make decisions about filling positions, those decisions are made with data and confidence, and not merely by the preference of the loudest person in the room. Also, because the hiring manager and recruiter worked closely from the outset on what were the key characteristics needed to fill the position, decisions happen faster and without the false starts that poor communication causes. Those decisions can also stand scrutiny because the process reduces bias.

C-Suite

The really big difference here is you have a level of confidence that you'll be able to hire the staff you need in order to make your numbers.

You have a detailed understanding of the talent plan, how the organization is doing against that plan, and clear expectations for what is going to happen next.

Part of the reason why you have all this good information is you've made a major effort to get visible about how hiring is crucial to the organization. No staff meeting happens without a discussion of hiring. The organization celebrates meeting its sales goals, but it also celebrates meeting diversity, equity, and inclusion (DE&I) goals and other hiring benchmarks. You expect all managers to be equally involved with hiring efforts and achievements.

Employees Who Refer Friends

It feels great to be able to actually help friends when they need it, and helping them with a positive job-hunting experience is a big deal.

Of course, the best outcome is when you refer a friend to an organization and the friend is hired. That's especially true when it's a good fit based on data and a thorough interviewing process. But even when your friend doesn't get the job, if it was a positive interview experience then everyone benefits to some degree.

Employees at organizations with great hiring practices become a legion of ambassadors, spreading the word to similar people, literally day and night after work.

"Yeah, right. In your dreams."

In this book, we're going to stop now and then to address a thought that we're pretty sure you may have at that moment. Right now we suspect that you're torn between being excited at the prospect of becoming badass at hiring—but you feel like your organization will rise to the occasion like a boat anchor. "Our organization is different," you say. "That might have worked before, but not in today's tough competitive environment," you say.

We are here to tell you that normal organizations have made this transformation in good times and bad. It's not, as they say, rocket science, nor is it fantasy land. It's actually pretty straightforward stuff.

If we're going to be blunt with each other, you better hope that you're reading this book before one or more of your main competitors does. If they actually read and adopt just a portion of these practices, they're going to kick your butt.

There's a catch, though.

Isn't there always a catch to things that sound too good to be true? So, here's the tough news about this opportunity:

To create hiring excellence in your organization, you as the leader will need to change.

As we said at the outset, this is a book for leaders of organizations, and leaders are extremely busy people. Be that as it may, you're going to have to get much more personally involved in hiring in order to pull this off.

Yes, you have a whole HR department whose job includes hiring. That should be enough, right?

Wrong. You have to become what we call a Talent Maker, which we will describe in much detail in Chapter 9. Your HR department needs you to step up and not just *say* but *show* that hiring is a priority. You need to create the space for people on your team to work *on* the business, as well as *in* the business, in order to effect this remarkable transformation.

In the years since we started our company, we've been on the lookout for magic bullets to make the change happen instantly and painlessly. Alas, so far we've only been able to find the next best thing: a proven method for putting in the time and hard work in order to create an additional major asset, namely your ability to hire great people at will. This book will show you how to do it.

If you would like to read about our backgrounds and how our experiences led to developing the Greenhouse approach for hiring great talent, then read on. Otherwise, if you're impatient to get right into it, you can turn to Chapter 2.

"So, the Greenhouse founders wrote a book about hiring. It's going to be one long sales pitch for their products."

We are extremely well-known in the recruiting world, and therefore, it's understandable to have HR folks associate us with being an ATS provider. In case you've never heard of an ATS, it's a common tool in organizations, and it does what it says: tracks the status of applicants, candidates, interviews, job offers, and so on.

Let's get something out of the way: We think we offer a great product, and it's much more than a mere tracking system. You can read all about it on our website. It can accelerate the transformation of your organization. We hope you try it. There, that's our sales pitch.

Back to this book: It is not about our software; it's about the principles of world-class hiring. You do not need our software to become amazingly good at hiring. You can use a free word processor and spreadsheets if you wish. That might not be the most convenient way, but it will work.

Let's put it another way: If you continue with your hiring mess and change nothing, and if your competitor implements just a fraction of what we'll discuss here but uses Google Sheets and Microsoft Word docs, you're in for some rough sledding. Instead, be that competitor who implements. If you want to activate a major hidden tool for organizational success, you don't need any software but you absolutely must become the Talent Maker and catalyst for your team.

Therefore, you'll hear us refer to Greenhouse a lot in this book. When we do, we mean our method and culture of hiring, not our software.

So, why isn't a great ATS the solution to great hiring? Because it's not about tracking poor behaviors better; it's about changing behavior.

It's about solving a different set of problems, which relate to how priorities are set, what actions get taken, and how decisions are made.

We actually had a competitor who at one point launched a whole advertising campaign. In effect they said, "Take the hassle out of hiring. We're going to make hiring so easy, you can finally get back to the real job of building your company."

That was both extremely funny and kind of sad at the same time. All organizations are built from three components: people, capital, and assets. The assets may take the form of intellectual property, machinery, raw materials, signed contracts, whatever. Of those three components, only one—the people one—can create the other two.

Hiring is the mother of all variables, the one that can boost performance to the moon or can crash a company in no time flat. And organizations hope to buy some ATS so they can get back to their *real* work? That's the attitude of the walking dead, and they don't even know it.

Unique Window

As we said, we have a window into the inner workings of organizations of all types, from the titans you hear about every day, to hyper growth start-ups, nonprofits, multinationals, and old-line established firms. Of course, we're very careful to protect confidentiality and obscure details when necessary. But in these pages you'll get insights that are almost impossible to get any other way: They represent many more experiences than any one person could have in a lifetime. They're more than a management consultant would have because they're rooted in the deep inner workings of thousands of organizations over many years.

Even so, please note that we do not have all the answers, and don't pretend to. We're merely on a journey to get better at hiring and to spread that culture to like-minded organizations with a willingness to listen, try things, occasionally stumble, and always pick themselves up. Including hiring in your core focus is unbelievably rewarding.

"But do we really need another book about hiring?"

Lots of books—including some good ones—talk about how to recruit: ten subject lines to lay on candidates to make them open your email, how to pitch a job, how to do a good interview, how to convince a candidate to take a job, and the like. It's at the practitioner level.

This is not such a book. As we said earlier, we want to have a discussion with leaders, whether they are the C-suite, a department head, middle manager, or team leader. We think a breakdown occurs in the interface between people who are tasked with recruiting, and those who are tasked with the business side and think they can delegate hiring to HR. We want to offer a proven framework for creating an internal alignment and commitment that works for everyone, and succeeds in attracting amazing talent.

If we do our job in this book, the head of HR and the CEO will give a copy to each other.

Companies need people more than ever. At the same time, people need companies *less* than ever.

Daniel: I graduated from a top engineering school in 1995. When I thought about my options for becoming a programmer, there was only one—work for a company. That's because there was no infrastructure for me to do my own programming work. Software tools cost $1,000–$2,000, and they ran on computers costing around $4,000. They had to be connected to a network running at a company, and remote work was not possible.

When I applied for jobs, I first went to the bookstore in downtown Ann Arbor and I bought a directory that listed the names of companies, their head of HR, and their mailing address. The problem was that the books were published by city. You thought about what city you might want to work in, and you bought a few of these books. There were no online job listings or much of anything online at the time. I had no idea what their salaries were, what the culture was like at the company, or even if there were any job openings to begin with. There were no postings in these books because of the lead time from when the companies submitted their materials and when the printer published and distributed the books.

Sure, I attended job fairs at my school, but only a handful of companies made it to those fairs, and even for those companies, information was scarce. In a real sense, the amount of information I had on a company was not much different from what one of Charles Dickens's characters had on a company in London in the 1800s.

Still, I felt pretty high-tech at the time because I didn't have to type out my résumé and application but could use a word processor! I printed the paper, stuck it in envelopes, and mailed it to companies. Outside of small networks where maybe a friend knew a friend who worked somewhere, I was completely at the mercy of what the company wanted me to know about it.

Let's compare that experience to someone graduating from school just 25 years later. I can easily strike out on my own with programming. I can log into GitHub for free and produce my own software. In fact, I have access to the most powerful design and programming tools in history and they cost me nothing.

I can instantly and immediately distribute my software anywhere in the world. It's my choice whether I charge for it, or give it out for free as a loss leader for the personal brand I might decide to build.

If I feel like exploring the jobs available to me in organizations, I have a global database of basically every white-collar professional at the click of a button. I can get the real-time lowdown from Glassdoor about what it's like to interview or work at any company, and it's uncensored.

I can explore different job openings by filtering as widely or narrowly as I wish. I can also check out job types that I would never have thought about pursuing, were it not for the ease of doing research now.

My word-of-mouth network is vastly larger, because it's so easy to see who are friends of friends and get introduced to them. I can instantly apply to crazy numbers of jobs, and in many cases work from the other side of the globe.

In short, I have astonishing amounts of information and transparency about the job market. In addition, tools make it possible for me to have side hustles or be self-employed full time if I wish from anywhere. The relatively recent days when companies controlled information and you had a choice of a handful of companies (or TV stations) is long, long gone.

People still do apply to jobs, but increasingly it's the jobs that are applying for people. Let's say someone is an engineer, logistics expert, or environmental attorney and starts a new user group on LinkedIn or somewhere else. For a little, while there will be only like-minded people in the group. Pretty soon a recruiter will sniff around, hear about the group, and get added. Secrets don't have a long half-life in recruiting, so before long a bunch of recruiters are in the group, spamming subject-matter experts with offers to interview.

It's true that jobs will often have dozens or even hundreds of applicants. But employers would be making a big mistake if they think that means they have all the power. First, the most competitive candidates have multiple job offers, as we mentioned earlier. Second, a lot of applications are submitted by robot, where someone can click a button and blast a résumé far and wide. Therefore, the number of qualified, desirable, available candidates is far smaller.

What we are seeing in organizations is there's a shift happening, where the head of sales and the head of engineering are increasingly realizing that the success of their own position is based on how well they hire *and retain* real talent.

Boards are also sitting up and saying things like "What *exactly* is your hiring plan for the next quarter and next year? Because if we extrapolate the lines on these graphs, you're not going to make your numbers without those positions being filled."

This system stems from the experience of a great many organizations.

Our approach to hiring is the result of the founders' experience and also the refinements and suggestions from our community. At the start of this book, we think it may be useful for you to understand the beginning of Greenhouse, and how it came about as a result of real-world hiring challenges.

> *Daniel:* I started a consulting company in the early 2000s. Our firm would hire programmers and put them on projects at banks. Early on we didn't have any brand or market power to speak of. What I did have was an engineering and programming background and I was extremely strict about the level of quality that we would accept for a programmer.
>
> Soon, we got a call from a big-name firm in Manhattan, and we had just the person for their needs. The bank would not take our word for it that our person could do the job, and they insisted

on interviewing him. I proudly sent our programmer to Midtown, knowing that he would blow the doors off the interview.

After a bit I contacted the client and was told, "Oh, yeah, we rejected that person." I'm thinking: *What? This guy was unbelievably good! Cream of the crop!* It made no sense at all. I asked the programmer what happened. He said, "I sat in a whiteboard room with some guy who was totally bored. He obviously had zero interest in being in the room, and barely looked me in the eye. He asked me the nit-pickiest little questions about some obscure, unimportant programming syntax that no one ever heard of or uses. Then the meeting kind of ended and he walked out."

Wow, that was weird. Hey, maybe it was bad chemistry, or maybe my guy said something that caused a problem, because it certainly was not his level of skill that could be the issue.

But it happened again—and again. And with different programmers and banks. I soon realized that at these big banks, they were just asking one of their programmers to do the interview and putting them in a room with no guidance or instruction whatsoever. The interviewers weren't asking questions that indicated they knew anything detailed about the specific tasks we were asked to find someone for. No one was invested in this; in fact, it could be that the programmer/interviewers might have been a little worried that our people could end up being their replacements.

While this puzzle was unfolding, I was hiring and scaling my own team. Frequently, I had two of my people interview the candidates. I remember on one occasion when I asked how things went, one of my guys said, "That was the best candidate I've ever met. You should not let this person out of the building without making an offer on the spot." I asked my other interviewer, who told me, "I'm not working with that woman! Do *not* hire her! Let me put it this way: If you put her on my team, I'm quitting!"

Am I in some kind of time warp? First, the banks make no sense with their response to fabulous candidates, and now my own team makes no sense! I knew both of my interviewers well and they were smart. I had to get to the bottom of this.

There was a Radio Shack in my building, so I went downstairs and bought two digital tape recorders. I gave them to my interviewers and asked them to tape all their interviews so I could listen to them on my commute to and from work.

I listened to a ton of interviews. It was probably a bad idea to be driving at the time because they melted my face. You cannot imagine how bad those interviews were. These were my own smart, hand-picked people, too! I had this epiphany: *Oh my God, I'm sending my people into these rooms, and I haven't told them anything useful.* Plus, I didn't give any instructions to the interviewers as a group, so I would hear four interviews of the same candidate by four different people. They all were asking the same questions.

Then the candidates would ask my staff questions. Some of my people would give terrible answers because they weren't trained or prepared. A candidate would ask, "So if I join this company, what will the projects be like?" And she'd hear, "Well, um, it kinda depends. Actually I was put on a pretty lousy project for all of last year. I know there's some good projects elsewhere in the company, but I'm not part of those."

Hence my melted face. *What are you doing? Are you trying to ruin my company?* After about ten miles I realized that it wasn't his fault. I didn't prepare him for that or any other question. He's a programmer! He was shooting the breeze about his own job, not interviewing someone for a different job.

Okay, I'm an engineer. This is solvable. No one knows what to do here, but it can't be that hard if we all sit down ahead of time. We can agree on what's important for the position and come up with a scorecard. If we care about these five or six criteria, what questions or tests could we come up with that will tell us if a candidate is a star, or okay, or terrible for those criteria? It could be as strict as a programming test for a programmer or as loose as "sell me this pen" for a salesperson. Let's also agree on who is going to ask which questions, so we cover everything on the scorecard. Engineers use data. We're going to collect all these data points, look dispassionately at the data, and use it to determine whom we hire.

That simple set of procedures made all the difference in the very next interviews we did. Night and day. It's one of those things where you think: *How could I have been such an idiot to not have thought of this before? And why are there so many other idiots doing the same thing, even in multi-billion-dollar organizations?* I didn't have an explanation, other than the blind leading the blind: "This is how we've always done it. It's how everyone's always done it."

Daniel and Jon met while in school. Jon's path had certain similarities:

Jon: I have a long history as a product manager. I worked at a company called BabyCenter back in 1997 when we were trying to figure out what the Internet was. After the company got bought, I became the first product manager at a company building performance management software for call centers, and then went to Johnson & Johnson, which had acquired BabyCenter and wanted to take it global.

The goal was to set up a media business with local pregnancy websites in 20 countries around the world. We'd launch a site, get a whole bunch of traffic, and then start selling ads against it. It was almost like a franchise model.

The big challenge was that we needed to find local editors in 20 countries around the world. Each editor in turn would need to hire a team—and all of this had to happen very quickly. So how were we supposed to find the best pregnancy editor in Rio, and Moscow, and Beijing, and Kuala Lumpur? We created a whole process around how we would advertise and network, then we planned how we would interview them, including testing their skills in their local language.

We were really under the gun and had to buy our plane tickets all around the world well in advance of even having any candidates identified in those cities. We developed a process so that when the time came to visit a city, we'd have four finalists to interview, we could make an offer on the spot, and get the training started. Then we'd move on to the next city. Our methodical process was good enough that 15 years later, I hear that some of the folks we hired are still there.

It's important to note that we built this effective recruiting machine even though we did not have an ATS.

Not long after, Daniel and I were both at crossroads in our careers. We'd had some interesting similarities in our experiences with hiring and we explored how we might capitalize on that in the form of a company.

We didn't start with the intention of creating an ATS; instead, we got out some index cards and mapped out the system we had in mind. It was everything we learned about designing a structured interview process.

We began to show our process to people we knew, one of whom was Fiona, a product manager at the *New York Times*. We showed her the steps, and the systematic approach to preparing interviewers, conducting the interviews, generating feedback, and making decisions based on data.

Fiona was like, "Wow, I never thought about it that way. This is easily the best plan I've ever seen for any hire and I'm actually going to use this." We were just in research mode at the time, but that was pretty encouraging feedback.

Daniel knew the founders of a start-up incubator in Manhattan and he offered to do a class on how to do a better job of hiring. They put it in their newsletter and the next day the room was jammed with 30 people. The discussion went on for three hours.

Then we started to get emails. More than one said words to the effect of: "I was in your class yesterday. I went into work on Monday morning, had a meeting with my exec team, and we changed how we hire—that same day. Thank you!"

Well, that was about all we needed to hear in order to get us moving ahead in earnest. We did the necessary things like write a business plan, incorporate, and raise money. Before long we were up and running.

For quite a while we had no sales team. The buzz we generated from doing a few talks was enough to get the phone ringing. Pretty soon we were doing 10 demos a day and the fish were jumping into the boat. In short order we went from our first 25 customers to getting 25 a month and then 25 a week.

Throughout this book, you will hear about organizations that have adopted a structured approach to hiring. Some of the best improvements we've made to the process have come from suggestions by our customers. All of us, including Greenhouse, are on a path toward continually improving at hiring. The great news is that once you're out of the quicksand that is hiring chaos, you can regularly see the progress you're making.

How We Structured the Book

We like to think in systematic terms and so we've structured this book to give you a logical framework for great hiring.

Part 1: The "Why"

Chapters 1 to 3 relate to the importance of great hiring. You've already gotten a 30,000-foot overview of the background that led to developing our approach.

Chapter 2 takes you through the Hiring Maturity Curve, which is a detailed way for you to understand where your organization is on the continuum from nightmare to dream. You may think, *Oh that's easy, we're a mess.* But it may be that certain parts of your organization are functioning at higher levels than others. We'll see.

Chapter 3 is about the Employee Lifetime Value (ELTV) model. What gets the focus and priority in organizations tend to be the things where a return on investment (ROI) can be measured, like salespeople, new products, and so on. We provide a way to think about hiring in more quantifiable terms.

Part 2: The "What"

Here is where we dive into the specific competencies of world-class hiring.

Chapter 4 introduces the framework we call "Structured Hiring" at what you might call the 5,000-foot view. It's the core of our approach.

Chapter 5 lays out the first competency, which is to "Own every moment of your hiring experience." This is primarily about the importance of breakthrough candidate experiences. We hope you will see the hiring process through a different, sharper lens.

Chapter 6 is Competency 2: "Identify and attract the best talent for your organization." This is, of course, a perennial problem for most organizations, but here you'll discover a more predictable way to get the candidate flow you need.

Chapter 7 is about Competency 3: "Make confident, informed hiring decisions." The only thing worse than not filling a position is filling it and then regretting it after a short, expensive time. That is much less likely to happen after you read this chapter.

Chapter 8 is Competency 4: "Use data to drive operational excellence and improve over time." Having the right skills and behaviors to attract great talent is critical. When you intentionally design these things into automated, measurable processes, you will get to the realm of amazing.

Part 3: The "How"

Chapter 9 is called "Talent Makers" and it's all about *your* potential. Some leaders do things very differently from you with respect to hiring. They spend their time differently, talk about different things, and have different priorities. As a result, they get different outcomes. The good news is you can also do those things and get those outcomes. We describe the three elements that can transform you into a catalyst for attracting and retaining the people who will propel your organization to achieve amazing things.

Chapter 10 covers the challenge of "Changing Minds." It's one thing for you to be convinced of the importance of becoming great at hiring. It's quite another to effect that change in an organization that's been doing things a certain way for a long time. We provide some approaches that have been effective in other organizations.

Final Thoughts wraps up the book with a couple of important recommendations for you, as you continue or begin your own transformation.

Expert Insights

Throughout this book, you'll see sections called Expert Insights. There we interview a number of recognized experts in different aspects of hiring. We think you'll find their experiences and observations to be practical and useful.

Structured Hiring Framework

We will be covering a lot of concepts in this book. As you read through the chapters, we thought it would be helpful to give you an overall framework for thinking about the major moving parts to structured hiring. You can see that framework in Figure 1.1.

Of course, this single volume cannot contain all the examples and resources that we've assembled to support the many concepts you'll

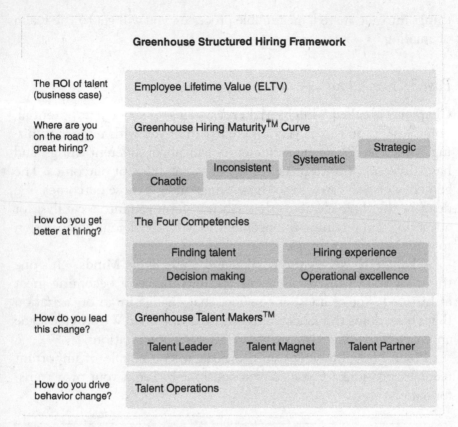

Figure 1.1   The Structured Hiring Framework.

read about. Therefore we'll occasionally refer to a companion site we set up at talentmakersbook.com/resources. You'll not only find those supplemental assets there, but we'll add new materials as the hiring landscape changes.

Let's dive in, shall we?

2

From Chaos to Confidence: The Hiring Maturity Curve

On the one hand, it's true that when it comes to hiring, organizations are all over the spectrum from ghastly to amazing. On the other hand, that by itself is not a particularly valuable or actionable insight.

What's more useful is first to understand what the spectrum is in the first place, and how to think about the different stages. Then it's helpful to examine four key competencies and how they look and feel across that spectrum.

By the end of this chapter, you'll have a type of identification kit, which you can break out at any time to assess the situation at your organization overall, or in any portion of it.

So what is this spectrum? We call it the Greenhouse Hiring Maturity Curve, and it looks like what you see in Figure 2.1. It's the result of observing the stages of the many thousands of organizations we've worked with.

The easy part is showing the curve. The harder part is explaining the nuances. To start, we have four stages:

Stage 1: Chaotic. Call it the Wild West, or a free-for-all, it's where hiring painfully gets done when circumstances force the issue.

23

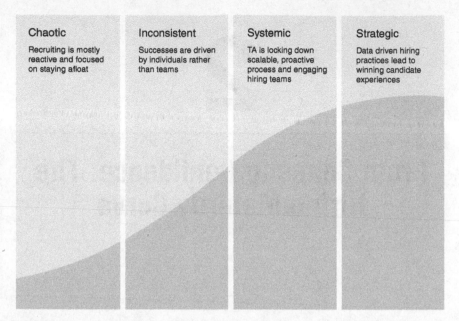

Figure 2.1   The Hiring Maturity Curve.

Stage 2: Inconsistent. There may be bright spots where hiring is working, but it's the exception rather than the rule.

Stage 3: Systematic. This is where organizations have their act together—where the machine can be counted on to work.

Stage 4: Strategic. Here's where organizations quickly pull away from the rest because they have the measurements, automation, and continuous improvement that allows them to hire great talent at will.

Of course, these are not sharply defined stages, but rather a continuum. When did an organization go from being Chaotic in Stage 1 to Inconsistent in Stage 2? In a sense, it doesn't matter precisely when it happened, because the usefulness of the curve is to have a way to find your bearings. It's also useful to have a graphic or description like this in order to start a discussion. If one person says, "Oh, we're killing it. We're easily at Stage 3," and someone else thinks we're barely out of Stage 1, now we have the jumping-off point for a useful discussion. Bring your examples and state your detailed case.

Warning: What you do not want to do is just launch into a discussion of "What stage are we in? 1.2? 1.5? . . . " Invariably, someone in the room will say, "We're now arguing about how many angels are on the head of a pin. This is all semantics. Can we get back to our real work now?" The model is now tainted with that dead-end discussion and future useful discussions around it are less likely.

It's better to keep any early discussion at a big-picture view. The first stage of any meaningful change is simple awareness, where we can find those bearings and have a vocabulary that's more nuanced than "We're messed up."

Never-Never Land

It's also important to set expectations properly at the outset. In our experience with organizations big and small, when a group is at Stage 1, it cannot imagine what it's like to be in Stage 4. The group might not even be able to imagine doing anything differently from the current bad situation: *It's always been this way, everywhere I've worked. Get over it and get on with the job.*

You can think of the Hiring Maturity Curve almost like a horizon, where people can see a little bit ahead, but the rest is beyond that horizon. It's therefore important for you, as a leader, to paint the picture of what it can be like over that horizon, but just don't use crazy bold colors that no one will believe are realistic. The goal first is to have the discussion, to get a common sense of where we are on the continuum, and to get us moving in the right direction. The good news is that when people have lived long enough in the lower stages of Chaos and Inconsistency, their idea of heaven is just to get one stage higher. They figure that Inconsistency beats utter Chaos every day, and there's some truth to that. This means that even some small wins early on will be met with enthusiastic relief. Just wait until they see the bigger wins.

Skills versus Competencies

Let's settle on another bit of nomenclature. A skill is something you get good at when performing a task. Someone may be great at designing graphics for emails such that they get opened and read by donors.

A competency is a larger set of knowledge, skills, and behaviors that combine to allow individuals—or groups—to be effective at executing complex processes. We are going to devote four chapters to the four competencies we mentioned at the end of Chapter 1. They're central to the discussion in this whole book, so we'll refer to them often. But for now, let's identify them in general terms again:

Competency 1: Hiring Experience

Own every moment of your hiring experience.

Competency 2: Talent Finding

Identify and attract the best talent for your organization.

Competency 3: Decision Making

Make confident, informed hiring decisions.

Competency 4: Operational Excellence

Use data to drive operational excellence and improve over time.

Cause and Effect

It's critical to understand that these four competencies are not outcomes the way Stage 1 Chaos is. The competencies are the drivers. They include not only the skills and knowledge, but also the behaviors of people. Therefore they determine where you are on the curve. You can see how this fits together in Figure 2.2.

Stage 1: Chaos

If you look at what leaders do in Chaotic organizations, there will be a lot of barking going on. Like every other organization, they need to make hires, but they have no clue how successful they're going to be. If past experience is any guide, their only clue is that it will be a miserable, drawn-out, expensive drama.

There is no transparency at this stage, so hiring managers are forever saying, "Where's my hire?" or "Why haven't we filled this seat by now?" Out of earshot of the recruiting folks, the questions are blunt and rhetorical:

- "What the hell are those people doing?"
- "We're paying them how much for these results?"

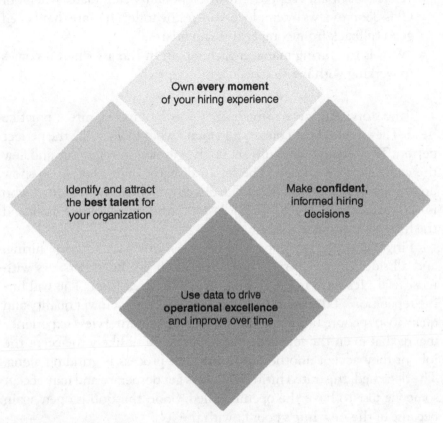

Figure 2.2 These Four Competencies Are Done Well—or Not—in Each of the Stages.

- "Why can't we seem to find any effective recruiters?"

While the business side of the organization is feeling that way, the recruiters have their own thoughts:

- "If they bothered to give me 10 minutes of information about the position, I could create a decent post. But no."
- "Why can't they tell me in detail what they don't like about this group of candidates, before I send them another?"

- "Exactly how am I supposed to attract quality candidates when our Glassdoor reviews by employees are in the toilet? It's rare that I even get a callback from competitive candidates."
- "Why is the hiring manager such a pain in the ass when it comes to working with me to schedule interviews?"

True story: An advertising agency was looking to hire a practice head. They scoured the country and found what looked like the perfect person. The recruiter carefully set up the whole interview day and flew the candidate to Chicago. The senior director didn't bother to show up to interview the candidate. The director blamed the recruiter, who in turn blamed the director; regardless, the candidate felt insulted, and the hire was not made that day.

Finger-pointing is rampant in organizations with Chaotic hiring, and all sides have plenty of ammunition to use on others. As with most feuds, it's hard to know what exactly started it all. The bad hiring reputation of the organization means that only a lower quality and quantity of people bother to apply. The horrible interview experience means that even the few decent applicants are unlikely to accept the job, or they accept another one while the process is grinding along. The detached, frustrated hiring managers get desperate and may accept someone just to have the opening filled. Soon that job is open again because of the new hire's poor fit with the job.

What the Hiring Experience Looks Like in Chaos

For starters, the job-application process is poor: you may be told to send your résumé to an email address; then again, a very widely used ATS requires people to retype their résumé into dozens of little text boxes, while you are praying that the system does not time out and boot you out, causing you to start over. (We've heard of applicants who swear that if they see a company using this brand of ATS, they will *never* apply for a job there.)

If you do manage to have your application submitted, you may hear nothing for a week, a month, or longer, if ever. (Far and away, the biggest complaint we hear from applicants is when organizations never bother to reply to an application—even if it's just to say, "Thanks, but no thanks.")

Let's say you get an interview. You're only told to show up at a certain time and place, with no other details about parking, with whom you'll meet, and so on. These days, when lots of interviews are being done remotely, you're not told whether it's a phone call or video session; you just get a link and will find out more when the session begins.

When you're sitting in the waiting room and you're not white, you might be asked why you're there. When the interview happens, often it doesn't start on time. ("Big deal. The candidates can wait. We call the shots.") Somebody plops down and starts to ask you disconnected questions, irrelevant questions, or downright illegal ones. The next person interviews you and you may get the same questions, as we mentioned in the last chapter. You're also likely to get completely generic questions, like "Please tell me about each job you've listed on your résumé," or everyone's favorite, "What are your greatest strengths and weaknesses?"

If you get a chance to ask questions, they may not know the answers to many of them. The interviewer may also have no clue about the technical terms you use when you ask questions about the position, because that person was not briefed at all on such details. When you ask what the next steps will be, nobody can give you any specifics because there are no specifics.

Things proceed extremely slowly. You could be asked to come back another time, not for a second, higher phase of interviews but because they didn't give you all the tests they could have the first time around.

If you happen to interview and are rejected, then often you'll be ghosted; it isn't on purpose but instead because the recruiter doesn't have a reliable mechanism for sending rejection notes.

You can be sure this assortment of lousy experiences will make its way to Glassdoor. It's only natural, like action-reaction: when you're treated carelessly or worse, you want to do something. It feels cathartic to write a "can you believe this" fresh, flaming account.

What Talent Finding Looks Like at the Bottom of the Curve

Daniel: When talking with a recruiter at a company that was struggling, I asked, "Where do you advertise your open positions?"

The person mentioned an ancient job board. I said, "Oh really? Why there?" The recruiter replied, "Oh, it's because they have this button in my ATS. I can literally make one click and buy an ad. So I push it and spend a hundred bucks. Done." That was the totality of their sourcing method.

Trust Is the Issue

The fundamental problem at this stage is a lack of trust between all parties. Hiring managers will say their recruiters are worthless. They don't trust that the recruiters will find the right candidate, so they hire their own staffing agencies and pay them from their own budget outside of recruiting. It happens all the time. Agencies capitalize on the fact that the hiring managers have given up on their internal recruiting team, and the agency fees sidestep any caps in the recruiting budget.

Once a prospect for our software asked for something that could only point to one thing in the organization—Chaos. She said, "I need to send my CEO a report every Friday that lists every single candidate that we interviewed across the whole company this week. I need to get it to her by 4:30 every Friday or I'm toast."

We work with a great many CEOs and I (Daniel) am one. There is only one reason why a CEO needs that level of detail in a report: The CEO has lost confidence in recruiting. The person thinks, *I'll micromanage and I'll do it better.*

Of course, the way to get out of this situation is not to say "no" to the CEO. That's a nonstarter. In the short term, you may have to send the report, but right away you need to be doing the things that will rebuild trust, so this person can relax in the confidence that the system will deliver.

We'll cover many ways to rebuild that trust. Explain to the CEO, "Here's how we're now going to agree on the criteria for a specific job; then here's how we'll divide up the interviews and cover all the bases in order to generate consistent data on all candidates. Then here will be our rating method. ..." Not only are you being proactive by doing that, but chances are good that the CEO will not have seen that level of structure before in any hiring process.

The lack of trust manifests itself in other ways. We'll sometimes see it come through in odd feature requests in our software. In one case, a recruiter wanted all sorts of buttons added so the hiring manager could review résumés faster. We dug a little deeper and found out that they posted a job and got around 100 résumés. The head of engineering was the hiring manager and his head was exploding at the prospect of reading 100 résumés.

We gently explained that the solution was not to have other buttons and features in the software; The problem was that the head of engineering did not trust the recruiter's judgment. He felt that the recruiter could not look at those résumés and make good decisions on his behalf. Just like the CEO above, he concluded that he had to do it all himself.

The solution was to have the recruiter and hiring manager agree on the specific criteria for evaluating those résumés. Is that outside the comfort zone of the recruiter for this particular, new type of technical job? Well then, the hiring manager's time would be better spent by getting the recruiter up to speed on the job details, how it's similar to and different from other recent jobs, what the terminology all means, what the true minimum requirements are, and so on.

Just think about the shift taking place here: The recruiter is going to delight the hiring manager by taking off his plate about 90 résumés for just this one job, never mind others. In turn the hiring manager will train the recruiter to become more knowledgeable about the true job requirements, which will pay dividends on this and other jobs down the road. A distrustful relationship can begin to be transformed into one where all parties are doing their highest and best work.

What Decision Making Looks Like in Chaos

The problem starts very early because there's no kickoff meeting to discuss the role. People are under the gun to hire someone and even if someone suggests a meeting, the likely reaction is "Look, I need someone fast. Are we going to sit around in another meeting, or are we going to get moving and post the job?"

They call this "parallel play" when it refers to toddlers: Everyone's sitting together but busy playing with her or his own toys. HR sends the recruiter a job description. The recruiter does her thing in a vacuum. The hiring manager is busy doing "real work" and just wants the seat filled. There's no discussion about what the key hallmarks of success are for this position, where we are going to find these people, or who will ask what during the interviews. Instead, someone might be working away and gets a tap on the shoulder: "Hey we got another candidate coming in; it's an hour from now in Conference 3. Go in there and tell me if they're good."

When the interviewer emerges, it's time to get back to work after that unplanned interruption. He may or may not bother to write an email to someone saying what happened in the meeting. After several candidates are interviewed that way, someone starts an email thread along the lines of "What should we do next?" It doesn't relate to where we are in the process and what's the next defined step; instead, it means "What should we do with this person? What do people think?"

Someone takes the predictable step of saying, "I'd like to see a few more candidates. Have any of them met with Terry?" Because everyone knows that Terry's ultimately the decision maker. When the time comes to make the decision, Terry may not even bother to review the "data" such as it is, on the candidates. (Terry would think, *Why bother looking at that hodgepodge of stuff? It's never helpful to me anyway.*)

If there ends up being a meeting to decide on who gets an offer, either people ask Terry for an opinion, or they just hang back until Terry speaks. *Why stick my neck out when we all know who's going to decide this one.* If some people do speak, it's stuff like this:

"Sally was really strategic; I think that would help our team."

"You mean the woman in the red outfit? Oh, I don't think she has nearly the experience of the man we saw yesterday ... Wakim? Joe-a-chim? Whatever it was. We need someone who can represent us better at trade shows."

Round and round it goes, until someone wants to see more candidates, or Terry makes a decision. No one leaves that room feeling like a solid process just happened.

Operations in Chaos

First, there are no systems that make the hiring experience easier for both the candidates and the organization. Applications may come in to different email addresses, and then are stored as attachments in someone's email account, or they may make it out of the account but some are then stored on someone's hard drive in HR.

Very few processes exist. Applications may get stored using haphazard filenames and multiple locations, so it's a pain just to find information. If someone who does know is out sick, the place grinds to a halt. Without a set of processes—even if they're just jotted down on notecards—people are left to improvise when it comes to how they'll generate sufficient applicant flow, conduct interviews, rate candidates, and so on. Without the processes, there is no shared vocabulary about the stage candidates are in and the tools we use.

Some processes may exist, but they're poor. For example, instead of having a meaningful discussion around what a position will entail, someone goes to Indeed.com and copies language from a sort of similar-sounding job. Done. That was easy!

Recruiting data doesn't really exist. It's a real pain to track the success rate of places where we posted jobs. No one thinks to look at the extent of diversity of the candidates at the top of our funnel, and then how that mix changes for who gets an interview, who's a finalist, and who gets an offer. Without such data, it's impossible to be in a position where you can sit up and say, "Hey, what's going on with this part of our hiring process? These numbers don't make any sense."

The organization does not live in its tools. Not only do few hiring-related tools exist, but even the spreadsheets are fragmented. Someone decides to start a spreadsheet because a tool doesn't exist, or is a pain to use. Someone else in the same department has a similar spreadsheet but not quite the same. Which one to use? Oh, and they're saved not online but as separate Excel files. Now which dated version of which person's spreadsheet is the one we need?

Being able to run queries against the data is exceedingly painful:

"I want to know what our average time to fill design jobs has been in the last three years. It seems like we're getting worse, not better. Am I right?"

"I'm not sure. You could be. Yes, it's technically *possible* for us to get that data, but you do know that it's a manual process, right? And that Wei-lin left a year ago and I don't even know how we're going to find where she stored those data. So, if you *really need* to see that data, I'm going to have to push back our Acme project date to make time to get it to you."

"Oh. Forget it."

If you walk through the recruiters' area, you'll see a million sticky notes posted everywhere. It's another vicious cycle: Our systems suck, so we don't use them. We instead need to create our own ways of tracking, which means the systems have no useful data.

Stage 4: Strategic Organizations

Note how we're jumping from describing what Stage 1 looks like and now want to focus on Stage 4. We'll come back to Stages 2 and 3 a bit later, but again, it's important not to get bogged down with overly detailed descriptions at each stage. The curve is most helpful when you have a good idea of what the bookends look like—the worst and best examples. Then it becomes easy to gauge where you are along that continuum.

Let's look at the four competencies at companies with great hiring.

What the Hiring Experience Looks Like in Strategic Organizations

Disney is a legendary company in part because of its relentless focus on the minutest of details. Other theme parks might be satisfied with staying somewhat clean. Disney monitors the humidity and temperature every night, so it can create the right formulation of paint in order to touch up railings *every night* and have them dry by morning opening.

Disney doesn't let you see the full length of a line you're waiting in, so you don't get depressed. Instead, there are little interesting things to look at as you wind around. And when you see a timer with an estimate of the line wait, the actual line is invariably a little shorter, so you feel good about spending less time than expected.

Companies with the best hiring practices have a similar attention to many details. Some go so far as to map out every interaction and then think about whether each spot could be done differently. For example, when people arrive in the interviewing room at Airbnb, they will receive a handwritten note, welcoming them.

How much does that cost in time or effort? But it's the kind of extremely rare touch that has a viral quality to it; you can bet that people are telling their friends about the Airbnb experience, and that's just one touch point of many they've mapped.

If the recruiter is conducting one of the interviews at a Stage 4 place, that person is fully up to speed with the common jargon for that position. The recruiter will be able to carry on a competent discussion about the details of the position, and how it may be different from other, similar ones. Right away the candidate will make a conscious note or have an unconscious sense that this is an organization that cares deeply about its people.

Of course, the recruiter might not be truly expert at any one job, but that's not the goal. Instead, it is to get a much higher quality of information from the candidate by using tailored materials and trained interviewers, and it's to make a much higher-quality impression on the candidate.

Remember that all the burden is not on the recruiter's shoulders to pull off a good interview. First, the interview kit is prepared so the recruiter has a script to follow. (More on that later.) Also, the right mix of interviewers will be carefully created so the truly in-depth specialized discussions can happen between the experts.

At the end of the interview, the candidate will have a crystal-clear idea of what the next steps are, and when they'll happen. The general impression is usually one of: *That was amazing. I've never experienced an interview like that in my life.*

What Talent Finding Looks Like in Strategic Organizations

Opening up a job in a Strategic operation looks different, right from the get-go. First, you have a comprehensive database of all previous and current applicants, candidates, and employees. You've already done some vetting on many of these people so you might quickly identify 15 candidates that way. Then you run a referral drive within the company and because you've put in the time to create a very active referral environment, you can identify another 15 diverse candidates with different backgrounds to enhance your search. Now, before you've done anything outside your organization, you've got a solid starting list of 30 or more candidates.

Then you have a surprisingly long list of places where you could potentially advertise the job and you choose a few or many, depending on the difficulty of filling the position. Because you have reliable data, you can make intelligent decisions about which media might be the best to advertise this particular job.

As we mentioned in Chapter 1, you don't just stick a dry job posting out there, but you create what reads more like an advertisement. The goal is to attract excellent candidates, and that often requires some persuasion.

What Recruiting and DE&I Look Like in Strategic Organizations

Organizations at this stage not only set targets, but they communicate those targets internally and publicly. They don't always hit them, but they're intentional and energetic about aiming toward them.

They might say something like "We expect that no more than 60 percent of our executive leadership will be male. To exceed California's legal requirements, we'll need two board members who are female and two board members who are people of color by the end of next year." They report on progress on those goals yearly or quarterly. They then design programs that make progress toward those goals.

Let's say that a company has the goal of increasing its number of female engineers. Campus programs often generate a relatively balanced gender mix and are a good place to focus for such jobs. They will visit colleges with strong female engineering programs. They'll send recruiters to speak to women-oriented engineering groups on campuses where for some time they've been developing relationships and supporting campus events. They encourage their senior female engineers to get the word out if they're visible on social media. These people often will have their own following and can regularly communicate what a great place the company is for women to work at. Even women who are not active on social media may have active personal networks, and they implore their female friends to work at the company because women are supported and have good opportunities to succeed.

Pipeline and Confidence

When an organization is at the other end of the spectrum, in Chaos, we've discussed how painful it is to source high-quality candidates effectively. When you do finally find a good candidate, you get so excited that you tend to stop sourcing others. If that candidate does get through the hiring process with flying colors, that's great. You've dodged a bullet. But the chances are excellent at Stage 1 companies that you've not snagged a world-class candidate, and that the person is less than meets the eye.

Now you're in a jam. You turned off your sourcing, and every day that unfilled job is costing you money. Can you even find another decent candidate soon? *Hey maybe this one is not so bad after all.* ...

Compare that to a Strategic situation. Not only do you have a much larger flow of candidates, but even after you identify some strong finalists, *you keep the pipeline flowing.* That gives you multiple options, so you don't have to pray that the one candidate works out.

Options give you confidence, and that comes across when you're talking with candidates. Options also enable you to move more quickly because if need be, you can pivot to someone else if the process bogs down for some reason with the first person. And if you're in the fortunate position of having more great candidates than you have openings, they will become some of those previously vetted candidates in your database for the future. Of course, a number of them will not wait around for your next opening and they'll instead be snapped up elsewhere. But some may be available down the road when you could use them. And their Stage 4 interview experience will have left them with positive memories of your brand.

Strategic organizations are in a whole different league when it comes to making offers. They have a much higher level of confidence because they have more candidates to choose from, and better data.

We had an opening a while back for an engineer. A really strong candidate interviewed with us and with another company. When we made her an offer, the candidate said, "You guys are offering me an Engineer Level 2 position. There's another company that's offering me Engineer Level 4. It pays more money and is obviously a better title. If you guys can match that, I'll work with you. I like what I've seen of your company, but if you can't match that, I prefer to take the other job because of the money and title."

We were able to come back to her and say, "Here's what we really liked about you. It's clear that you're good at A and B. But as we assessed you, we found that you really don't have much experience with C. You kind of missed the boat a little bit on C. We also think that D is a growth area for you. So here's our plan: If you decide to take this job, you'll come in at Level 2, and we're going to work with you on these factors. We think you could be at Level 4 in around 18 months. Here's how we'll get you there. ... "

She took our job. She actually agreed with our assessment, and it was obvious that we had put a lot of thought into her as a candidate and as a potential employee.

Sometimes, when you have this sort of conversation with candidates, it's not about skills. It could be that you're talking with a candidate who has all the skills but is weighing different offers. You know you can't match that other offer in terms of money, but you can offer faster advancement, more stock options, or the opportunity to work more flexible hours. The key is to have an amazing Stage 4 interview experience where you not only evaluate the person, but you listen actively and learn something about the person's motivations. From the outset you're demonstrating that you care much more than "can you do the job for this amount of money?"

You may or may not be into college basketball, but it's worth knowing something about Kentucky. Out of about 350 schools in the country, Kentucky gets an outrageously high percentage of the top players every single year. These players stay for a year or two, and then they turn pro and leave. So here you have a situation where basically all their stars leave. For most types of organizations, having all the best talent walk out the door would be cause for panic and maybe a board of inquiry.

Not for University of Kentucky (UK). It has such a strong program, with a culture and brand that attracts talent from all over, that it's just fine with turnover. Kentucky's a talent factory, and that's not a bad model to keep in mind when striving to become a Strategic organization in your own field.

What Decision Making Looks Like in Strategic Organizations

Your judgment can never be better than your information. The delays and hand-wringing that occur in Chaotic organizations are not the result of people who somehow inherently move through life more slowly. In fact, the opposite may well be true: They're scurrying around, trying to keep all the plates spinning, and it's not looking good.

On the other hand, a Strategic organization again has confidence because it's following a system, and the system works. The hot tempers don't manifest themselves as "What have you been doing! Where's my hire?" Instead they may look like "Why are you wasting our time at this meeting when you're the only one who didn't fill out the scorecard?"

Being a Strategic organization does not mean that everyone robotically agrees. There can still be heated discussions about which candidate is best. But those discussions are based on a full set of data: All the questions were asked, all the tests were administered and scored, and all the interviewers recorded their recent impressions before they conducted the next interview. Oh, and all those scorecards should get filled out before anyone can see others' scorecard ratings. Your scorecards should reflect what you think, not what you think others think.

Now you have a basis for a quick, effective discussion. There may be easy consensus on many criteria, with almost identical ratings. But a few things will jump off the page: Here we have four interviewers rating the candidate as quite low, yet one person gave a strong positive. What's up here? Or it could be that two interviewers seem much more positive across the board than everyone else.

Far from dreading the useless "What did you think?" type of sessions, these data-driven meetings feel like proper work is being accomplished.

Another win-win is how quickly the decisions can happen. With a well thought-out kickoff meeting, people make sure that all the data will be collected, and that reduces the chances of having to schedule a callback. There may be a second round of interviews, but it won't be because someone forgot to give a test or someone else couldn't be bothered to show up. Strategic organizations take hiring seriously so people know to make time on their calendars for interviews and other meetings, rather than procrastinate and finally agree to a couple of times two weeks from now.

Because decisions get made based on data, not only can they be made more quickly, but they're likely to result in more candidates accepting. As we saw earlier in this chapter with the Level 2 engineer, you have a solid basis for making the offer. You're much less likely to be lowballing the candidate.

Operational Excellence in Strategic Organizations

Operations is the framework that keeps all the hiring gears meshing with each other, and a lot of that framework is made of data.

At this stage, an organization can rely on predictive data. When we open the job, based on our well-organized data from many prior jobs, we know how many advertising outlets and sourcing activities we'll need to get the candidate flow we want. We'll also know how many candidates we'll need in order to find a great one, based on past jobs. We'll adjust our DE&I efforts because our data indicate that this job will be particularly challenging to get the right candidate mix. Therefore, we'll also be able to give the hiring manager a heads-up that the expected timeline will be a little stretched out on this one. Everyone knowing that up front means that no one is prematurely anxious.

Transparency is another hallmark. Everybody in the company knows what's happening and can see how it's going at any time without asking someone for an update and waiting for a reply. On key milestones there's external transparency with applicants and candidates.

Some organizations, like the e-commerce company Wayfair, are highly sophisticated, with data scientists and software engineers right on the recruiting team. They even have product managers on the team, focusing on the hiring experience.

"I don't have the luxury of being able to afford such specialists to improve my operation."

That would be the wrong takeaway from our description. First, you don't need to be huge in order to think about the applicant and candidate experience and make it better than it is today. Second, some of these organizations get big because they started to take hiring seriously when they were small, and it's paid dividends ever since. You do what you can with what you have—and even small operations can create a culture where you focus on the hiring experience, do better sourcing, make data-driven decisions, and tie together your systems such that you're measuring and improving continuously.

One way that Strategic organizations continuously improve is by experimenting. They may split-test how a job posting is written in order to measure if there's a statistically significant improvement in one of the variations. If so, that knowledge gets recycled into future postings, which will get tested in yet other ways.

Characteristics of the Inconsistent and Systematic Stages

As we've seen, when you're in Chaos, basically nothing works. When an organization moves to Inconsistent, it does have some successes, but they're individual and not Systematic.

Somebody may have a decent track record at hiring for a particular type of job. Maybe Alice is a very active alum at her school and over time has developed a steady pipeline of successful hires from that school. More power to Alice, but with a couple of caveats: First, that pipeline may be composed of people who are fairly similar to Alice, which may or may not be in the direction of the current DE&I hiring goals. Second, the pipeline is Alice's, so if she's not around, that source may dry up. None of that means that Alice should stop the good work she's doing; it only means that we're looking at Stage 2 here with little pockets that are working, but no organization-wide consistency.

It's like what you could imagine was the situation before Henry Ford came along. You might have been able to find craftspeople who were fabulous at building cars and others who could hardly tie their shoes. Not only is that an unpredictable way to create things, but it's difficult to scale. That's inconsistency.

Along came Ford, who standardized the assembly line. Now processes became easier to measure and best practices were easier to standardize. He took his company to Systematic. There was a Ford Motor Company way of doing things.

We don't mean to wade into a debate about assembly-line methods versus one-piece-flow systems. Instead, we're making the simple point that when there is a repetitive process like hiring, an organization improves when an anything-goes mentality is replaced by procedures and a common vocabulary. Then you can apply tools and measurements, and eventually develop Stage 3 Systematic procedures.

Certainly, it's not the case that an entire organization moves from one stage to another at one time. Some subgroups will always be ahead or behind others. People may be hired from companies that had excellent systems in place, so the new hires are true believers in those methods. They saw the benefits with their own eyes, can champion that approach in their new job, and can set up their area quickly.

Others will be the opposite. They'll be the last to change, may actively resist it, and will only comply while kicking and screaming. They may surround themselves with a blanket of excuses: "It'll never work," or "we tried it once and it was a waste of time," or "I've got more important things to do," and so forth. In Chapter 10, we'll discuss methods of accelerating positive change in an organization.

Also be aware that an organization may be Chaotic when it comes to one competency, and quite good in another. Again it could be due to an influencer within, who's a champion for the hiring experience, for example. That will pay immediate dividends in terms of the organization's brand and also the data on which to base hiring decisions. Even so, hiring decisions might still be in the stone age, depending on the power dynamics at work.

Over time, each competency can reinforce the others and the time invested in them will pay off. It's then that people "get it." Real change gets embedded in the organization when people in the trenches look at each other and say, "We're not going back to the old way."

No Excuses

In our experience with several thousand organizations, we see no correlation between the size of the operation and where they are on the Hiring Maturity Curve.

You may recall that in the last chapter we said that when Greenhouse was just starting, we gave a presentation at a start-up incubator.

Some of the attendees immediately implemented our approach. If they really followed through and embedded the principles of structured hiring into their companies, then they'd be good examples of being at Stage 3 or 4 while still being small.

Then again, we've found that some of the largest organizations—with all the money in the world—are squarely placed in Stage 2, with inconsistent practices. Sometimes aspects will verge on the Chaotic.

It's always so convenient to look at the neighbors' grass:

- "It's easy for that organization to have great hiring practices; just look at the kind of money they have."
- "We've become such an enormous company. Forget about 'turning on a dime' the way those startups can do; we're about as nimble as a battleship."

You can make excuses for not moving along the Hiring Maturity Curve, but you really have no excuses. Size doesn't matter, nor does capitalization, what part of an economic cycle we're in, the nature of your competitors, or your profit margins. What matters is whether you have the ability to keep the operation moving, doing the day-to-day stuff of working in the business. Then, will you force yourself to step back and work on the business, building the culture and the systems so you're steadily getting better at being able to execute? The speed at which you get better actually does not matter nearly as much as moving in the right direction.

Online Assessment

From what we've discussed in this chapter, you may already have formed an opinion about where your organization—or parts of it—falls on the Hiring Maturity Curve. To give you additional perspective on that topic, we have a 12-question online assessment. It only takes about five minutes to complete, and if you have multiple people take the assessment, it may form the basis of an interesting and useful discussion. You can find it at greenhouse.io if you type into the search bar "Hiring Maturity Assessment."

Chapter 2: Takeaways

All organizations are somewhere on the Hiring Maturity Curve, which has four stages:

Chaotic: Recruiting is mostly reactive and focused on staying afloat.

Inconsistent: Successes are driven by individuals rather than by teams.

Systematic: talent acquisition (TA) is locking down scalable, proactive processes and engaging hiring teams.

Strategic: Data-driven hiring practices lead to winning candidate experiences.

These are not four sharply distinct stages but instead are on a continuum. Organizations may have areas that are ahead of other areas. The size of your organization does not dictate where you are on the curve.

There are four competencies that are the drivers of where an organization falls on the Hiring Maturity Curve:

Competency 1: Hiring Experience
Own every moment of your hiring experience.

Competency 2: Talent Finding

Identify and attract the best talent for your organization.

Competency 3: Decision Making

Make confident, informed hiring decisions.

Competency 4: Operational Excellence

Use data to drive operational excellence and improve over time.

Expert Insights: Shauna Geraghty

Shauna Geraghty is Senior Vice President, Head of Global People and Operations at Talkdesk, a company with a valuation over $3 billion. She was the first US employee at Talkdesk and has helped to scale the company to more than 1,200 employees. Shauna has a doctorate in clinical psychology and has applied foundational knowledge from the field of psychology to help propel Talkdesk along its hyper-growth trajectory.

Talkdesk is a high-growth company. How did you go about hiring your TA team for this type of growth?

In 2016, we had 120 people in the company but no talent acquisition (TA) team. I was asked by the then COO to transition from my position within marketing to be Head of Talent. During the first month, I created my talent plan, which serves as the framework for our TA process and strategy today. This included the standardized recruitment process, standardized talent workflow, optimization of the Greenhouse software, creation of training for recruiters and hiring managers, creation of a wiki that documented the process, a framework for metrics and reporting, and a talent-marketing plan.

During this time, I was the first and only recruiter. I didn't make my first hire until the middle of that first year, in the talent operations function. My second hire was a senior recruiter. We brought 74 people into the organization within that first year, most of whom were senior and strategic hires. So it wasn't easy.

You have created a culture where people follow the hiring playbook. As we understand it, all hiring managers globally follow this process. In fact, if someone deviates from the process, it is typically a peer, not recruiting, that orients them back to the process. How did you create this type of environment?

It all goes back to the rigor with which we developed our standardized process, as well as the training and dissemination plan. We spent one year training the entire company about the process, and we trained adherence to this process. It took us that full year to make it from the bottom of the Hiring Maturity Curve to somewhere closer to the top of the curve.

Once the company was trained to adherence, hiring managers understood that following the processes created more velocity of candidates through the funnel and resulted in higher-quality hires. We were seeing results. So if a new hiring manager comes onboard and wants to use an agency, typically a peer or someone within the team will say that we don't use agencies, nor do we need them because everything is handled by our internal talent teams. That year of initial investment in training—helping our hiring managers understand the process—has paid dividends.

How does recruiting international talent affect the way you hire?

We have three global talent leaders and one leader of talent operations. We actually don't deviate from our standardized process based on geography. All candidates have the same experience regardless of their location. There are micro changes that we have to deploy; for example, certain questions aren't appropriate to ask in certain regions. But, in general, we have the same process globally.

The reason that's important is every single one of our departments has a global function, with employees across the world. Hiring managers might be located in San Francisco, but they might be paired with a recruiter in Lisbon. They need to be able to speak the same language, quite literally, but also all understand that we're running the same recruitment process. Whether they're looking for talent in Lisbon, San Francisco, or a remote location, those candidates will have the same experience.

We understand that the very first hire you made in your department was a Talent Operations person. Most companies first hire recruiters. Eventually, when they're at 750 to 1,000 people, they'll hire a Talent Operations person. That person then has to come in and clean up a mess. Getting an ops person first is a very different mindset, right?

Absolutely. That was critical to executing on our Talent Plan as they own our systems and tools, data integrity, metrics and reporting, vendor relations, talent marketing, talent nurturing, talent team training, interviewing logistics, and talent coordination. Building all this while being the only recruiter was tough, but it allowed me to put together the business justification to bring on a Talent Operations resource. Our CEO and COO knew it would allow us to build a solid foundation from which we could scale.

When you are a team of one, what do you do to start creating a culture of structured hiring?

In addition to developing a comprehensive process with rigor as well as a comprehensive training and dissemination plan, we also included key moments within the process that facilitated alignment with the process. For example, after a position has been approved by finance and our executive team, the next step is to hold a new position kickoff meeting. This is an opportunity to discuss all the components of the process, such as a hiring plan, competencies or scorecard constructs, ideal candidate profile, target list creation, outreach messaging, screening questions, and hiring manager meeting cadence.

Not only does this process allow recruiters to position themselves as a strategic business partner, but it also functions like a contract. So, if conversion rates throughout the funnel are atypical, a recruiter can use the information captured in the new position kickoff to drive better alignment or make strategic changes to the criteria to produce results. Also, during the debrief, if someone on the interview team discusses whether a candidate is a good fit for the role based on something that wasn't defined in the new position kickoff meeting, that document can empower a recruiter to facilitate a discussion with the interview team about hiring criteria. This ensures we're aligned before kicking off a role and that we stay aligned throughout the process.

3

Employee Lifetime Value

What are your top performers worth? We don't mean what you're paying them, but what they're *worth*. Better yet, what ROI are you getting on them? You might be able to answer these questions if those people are in sales, but how about for the many other roles? If you struggle with these questions, then this chapter will provide some clarity.

Most leaders believe talent is important, but in concrete terms they cannot figure out precisely what great hiring is worth to their companies.

In a sense, that's understandable. If I buy a piece of equipment, I should be able to calculate what it will produce for me over time, or the cost savings it may create over its useful life. If I advertise on Google, I can measure in real time what are my clicks, conversions, revenue, and ROI.

But hiring creates this odd paradox. On the one hand, many organizations say things like "People are our most important asset," yet they don't have a clue about how to calculate any overall ROI for that "most important" asset.

It's true that they know pieces of the equation. They know what it costs to hire people, but they often don't know what they're worth. In this situation, organizations tend to focus on costs.

One way they do this is to copy what high-profile companies do. For example, Google has been known to up the ante in the perks war by first having top chefs, and then things like free dry cleaning, dog sitters, and so on. All these costs can be easily quantified and the unspoken logic is:

- Google's a great company.
- Google offers all these perks and lots of people want to work there.
- If we offer the perks, people will want to work here.

This logic only gets reinforced as the perks war intensifies.

These high-profile bidding wars with amenities sometimes have the opposite effect on companies: they regard the perks as nonsense—or as impossible to quantify—and pull the plug on ones they installed.

As we'll see in this chapter, both copying and underinvesting can be wasteful and wrong.

A useful framework for getting a handle on both costs and revenues associated with someone's employment is something we call Employee Lifetime Value (ELTV). To explain it, let's first look at its well-known cousin—customer lifetime value.

Many companies calculate what a customer is worth on average, based on how much the customer spends over time with the company. Therefore, a marketing person knows how to make a pitch to the boss: "If I can get that proposed budget increase, then I'll be able to boost our number of marketing leads from 50K per year to 100K per year."

The same process works when the CTOs say they have found a way to slash the usual 12 months to complete a product roadmap, and will do it in half the time—if they can get funding. Those can be quick conversations.

We have to get HR conversions to the same place. Typical remarks made to the exec team today are hardly models of powerful logic:

- "We need to hire more."
- "We're swamped."
- "If only we had more people, we could ... "

The good news is there's a far more convincing way to discuss HR proposals in a way that speaks the language of ROI. As you will see, we will not have to calculate with great precision what each employee is worth to the company, in order to get the general idea that there is a positive ROI on the activities we're discussing in this book—how to get great at hiring.

Let's therefore go back up to the 30,000-foot level and look at some broad concepts about employees and how to think about their value over time. Take a look at the graph in Figure 3.1.

Time is going across the horizontal axis and the output of your employees is on the vertical axis. Don't worry about exactly what output is being measured. The point is that when you make a hire, you know that over time the employee will be contributing value. That was the whole reason for making the hire, after all.

When you actually hire the person, we're in negative territory, in the sense that there was an initial investment, with no return just yet. We had to advertise the job, interview them, hire them, get them equipment and initial training, and so forth.

At some point we start onboarding them, and the person ramps up to become a fully contributing employee, generating positive value for the company. Over time, they continue to generate value. The line may go up or down a bit, but you get the idea.

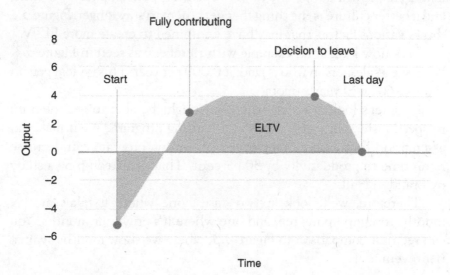

Figure 3.1   The Employee Lifecycle.

Eventually, the employee either decides to leave, or something else happens such that the employee won't be working there. So either suddenly or gradually, the employee's value contribution drops.

The shaded area under the curve is the total of the employee's contributions over time, and you have to net that against the initial region below zero and above the curve. That area represents the costs to acquire the employee. The sum of those two areas is the Employee Lifetime Value (ELTV). A goal of the business is to maximize the ELTV that you're getting from each employee.

What Affects the Shape of the ELTV Curve

How then do we maximize that ELTV? First, we can be more effective at sourcing. If we've cultivated our brand and done things like campus activities, blogging, meetups, referrals, and so on, we can lower the talent acquisition (TA) (talent acquisition) costs compared to a company that simply hired an agency.

We can also get the employee to ramp up more quickly by having better onboarding. We can affect the curve if we find more productive people, or if we have them working on higher-yield activities. Better management will get people to improve their performance over time, and a better culture is the thing that gets them to stay longer. Figure 3.2 shows various factors that may have combined to create more ELTV.

Let's now look at an example with numbers, as seen in Figure 3.3. We have a salesperson who is paid $60,000 per year. This typical person is on a $600,000 yearly quota.

Now let's look at a case where we might be able to get them up to speed faster, through a better onboarding program. We'll make an assumption that a better employee onboarding program can decrease ramp time to productivity by 30 percent. That's backed up by a study by Brandon Hall.[1]

Therefore, we'll look at two cases: one where it takes me six months to ramp up my rep, and one where it's only four months. You can see that comparison in Figure 3.3, where we show months against net revenue.

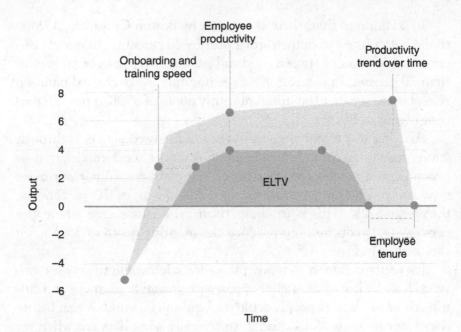

Figure 3.2   Some Factors That Increase ELTV.

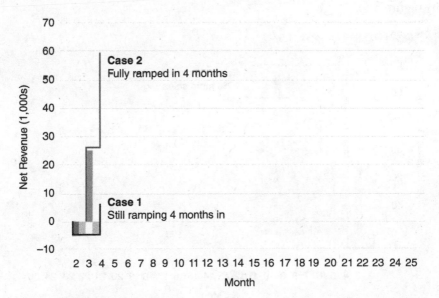

Figure 3.3   Speed to Ramp-up.

In addition to that, there is research by Boston Consulting Group that a better hire can outperform a peer by 20 percent.[2] In our experience, the difference between good and great sales reps can be far greater than 20 percent. In Figure 3.4, we see not only the decreased ramp-up time, but we see that the initial monthly quota of $50K is now 20 percent higher, at $60K.

Another way to enhance ELTV, as we discussed above, is through strong management and development practices. Let's model that as becoming not twice as productive as their plan, but 20 percent more productive. They overperform their $60K quota by 20 percent, so they're at $72K. This is in comparison to our base case where the person simply continues to produce the monthly quota of $50K. You can see this in Figure 3.5.

It's pretty common in many places for salespeople to stay for two years. If we look at what might happen with great management and culture, those productive people could stick around for another year before they leave for better jobs. And if we compare what happens when we have a productive employee who sticks around, versus needing to start the whole process over again, we see further ELTV differences, as shown in Figure 3.6.

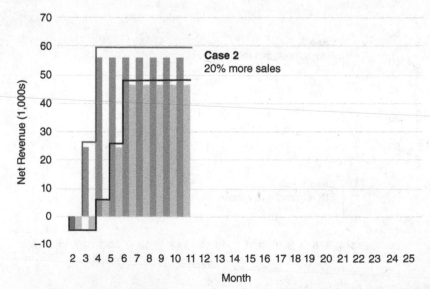

Figure 3.4   The Next Difference: A Better Hire Can Outperform a Peer by 20 Percent.

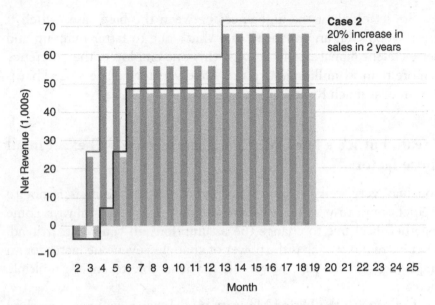

Figure 3.5 The Next Difference: Simply Higher Productivity.

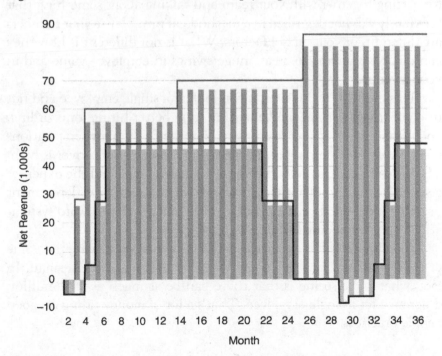

Figure 3.6 3-Year Overview with All Factors Present.

So, let's look at the differences between the base case, which is pretty good, and an enhanced case that's due to faster ramp-up and better talent management. For just this one employee, the difference is more than $1 million in extra revenue versus the base case. That is 2.5 times as much ROI.

"Yeah, but it's a fairy tale that a salesperson will excel in all those factors.'"

You may very well be right. The purpose of this analysis is not to predict some rosy scenario where all of these factors always come together. Feel free to change the assumptions all you want. Instead, what we're illustrating is the power of changing even one factor for an employee, and the superpower when you're able to engage multiple factors.

Just as with the Hiring Maturity model, you now have a method for getting together with your team and talking about something that previously was not described in a methodical way. Maybe your numbers are different, or your mix of factors. What is not different is how they can quickly combine to create huge swings in employee value and in your revenues.

This model is useful even if you look at a single employee and not in comparison to someone benefiting from better hiring, onboarding, and management. It's eye opening to view the ELTV hit when positions go unfilled, if onboarding is molasses-slow, and when turnover is high. Those positive areas under the curve get pretty small and the expenses get significant. Just quantifying the current situation for a department or for your organization as a whole will be a major start toward systematically understanding ELTV in your shop.

Keep in mind that just because the numbers quantifying the value of the better hire may be vague, that does not make them small. In fact, what we're seeing is that there can be as much as a $1 million difference for a single employee. That's a lot of money riding on good people practices.

The Hire as an Investment

The other big takeaway with this framework for quantifying ELTV is you should think of each hire as an investment. In fact, a hire is really a series of investments involving finding the applicant, screening and hiring the candidate, and ramping up that person. Then the ongoing investment happens in managing and regular training.

These investments need to pay off. We spend a lot of time with customers and in presentations at conferences on this concept of employees as business assets. We've found that a lot of HR people don't fully understand the dynamics on the business side, and many businesspeople are in the same situation with HR. That's OK; amazing power can be unleashed when that divide is bridged and paved with ELTV discussion, allowing for much higher levels of communication.

At the end of the day, hiring is a business decision and businesses need measurements. The whole coronavirus mess highlighted the need for businesses to use ELTV in their analysis. If organizations were not hiring during the pandemic and the CEO was considering slashing the HR department by 50 percent, just what were they losing? HR tends to have a really hard time answering that question, other than in general terms. Salespeople can talk about quotas and everyone gets that. But an HR area that does not make an ELTV case is on the chopping block, because maybe we should cut something with an unknown downside instead of something with a known one.

The Business Case for HR

Remember all those factors we overlaid on the charts above? The business case for HR to exist—and to potentially thrive—is to focus like crazy on those variables and move them in the right direction.

- How can we source more efficiently?
- How can we reduce our onboarding time and get to full productivity faster?

- How can we hire, such that fewer people leave due to a mismatch?
- How can we hire differently so we get the power boost from top performers versus average ones?
- How might we improve our referral program and thus gain a double-barreled advantage: another good sourcing avenue, and an environment where people stay longer because their friends work there?

In addition, each of these points can be broken down, fractal style, into subpoints to work on, and they all can boost ELTV. When we look at the one question above about how we can source differently, we can then ask:

- What investments are we making today that can have a long-range payoff? For instance, supporting campus programs, or having someone begin to write regular blog posts, or create meetups?
- What have been our most productive sources for candidates when we need to boost our DE&I efforts for a particular role? How recently have we researched whether similar sources may be out there to the ones that have been most effective?
- What is the nature of negative reviews relating to our interviewing process, and are any of those reviews both valid and readily solvable?

When HR works on projects like these and ties the efforts directly to the ELTV concept, now the CEO will have much more to consider before concluding that an HR staffing cut will make no difference.

The ROI of Copy and Paste

Let's go back to the typical situation we mentioned at the beginning of this chapter—the copy-and-paste approach to adding benefits. Somebody says that in order for our engineering department to keep and attract talent, we need to hire a private chef.

Let's think about that in ELTV terms. We determined that a private chef of the quality we want will cost $80K per year, and the food they will cook will cost around $1 million per year. Our hypothesis with the ELTV curve is that this may have no effect on factors like onboarding, but that the chef may result in our engineers staying 20 percent longer. That may translate in an organization to a value of $4 million, in which case you should consider the business proposition. If you follow through, you will then have data about attrition as well as survey data that may or may not support that hypothesis. We're now in territory that's more quantifiable than "Let's hire a chef, 'cause that's what everyone's doing."

If we think that by hiring an extra recruiter we could fill our jobs 10 percent faster, that's worth considering. If we know that every day we don't fill a particular role it costs us $3,000 in sales, again we have a quantifiable test we can consider, as well as the quantified daily pain while that role goes unfilled.

Let's look at the analysis from a different angle. If we know the daily lost revenue of a certain role, and we know the cost of hiring an extra recruiter, we can solve for how much faster we need to be able to hire in order to break even with that recruiting hire. If the analysis indicates that we only need to achieve a 4 percent decrease in time to fill a job in order to pay for the recruiter, now we have more information with which to make the decision.

Please note that this kind of analysis not only brings more clarity to hiring decisions, but it also brings accountability. If HR gets the additional staff or the chef gets hired, now the experiment is running. It's sometimes the case that the harsh light of accountability is uncomfortable for units that have traditionally not been measured in ROI terms. But it's also true that traditionally, some HR areas have clamored for a seat at the table. Well, ROI is what they talk about at that table. You want a seat there? ELTV is the ticket.

"You don't have a $20,000 problem; you have a $100 million problem."

Daniel: Early on we spoke to a prospect that was a tech company on a fast track to an IPO.

When I went to pitch them, they were around 275 employees. As I talked I could see that their recruiters were loving our software. They were having these aha moments left and right. They were saying stuff like "This is great!" and "Awesome!" followed by "Send us your proposal."

(continued)

(*continued*)

I sent my proposal. It was like $20K a year. They completely freaked out in the bad sense of the word. I was shocked, and called my contact: "What's the issue?"

It turns out they had been using a cheapo startup ATS, and were spending $1,800 a year on it. My contact said, "Listen, Daniel. Greenhouse looks amazing. I totally get it. All the features are awesome. You guys seem great. I could totally go to my CFO and tell them I need $2,000 more than we're paying today for a better tool. Maybe even $3,000 more. But you're asking me to pay *ten times as much*? That's insane. Are you crazy?"

I said, "Look, you guys are building a public company now, am I right? You have 275 employees and based on your own data, you've got 30% employee turnover. From what you've told me, you need to hire a net new 200 to 300 employees a year for the next five years. The result is that either you will have created a multi-billion-dollar public company, or you'll be one of the many companies on the trash heap of history that never made it."

I continued, "Billions and billions of dollars literally hinge on the next few hundred people you hire. So in that context, do you think it's worth the $20,000 investment? Is your CFO really going to question the $20,000 if they could put their thumb on the scale and give themselves a 5 percent better chance of building the right company?"

We got the sale. It was a whole different lens through which to look at these types of problems. We were not offering an ATS with some better features; we were offering a solution to one of the company's core challenges and most valuable financial investments—its people.

It Opened Their Eyes

Jon: There's an ad agency in New York City. It's pretty big, with around 1,000 employees. They had a series of brown-bag lunches for their HR team, and they invited me to present. We got to talking about possible topics, and they loved the idea of discussing ELTV.

I showed up to the lunch and they had around 40 people in the room or dialed in from around the world. It soon became apparent that they had also invited some finance people. I got them up to speed on ELTV and we had a lively discussion. Afterward I spoke with the organizer and found out that the entire event was put on for an effective target audience of two of the people in the room—the finance folks.

The HR area had been having a very hard time communicating to the finance people why they wanted to make certain changes to how they ran their people practices. The finance team was just not listening, or if listening, they were immovable.

The behind-the-scenes subject at hand was the question of whether the company should take the days off between Christmas and New Year's. The finance folks were like "Are you insane? That's five billable days. We're not doing that." In other words, a known cost and an unknown benefit.

When the company now had a framework for discussing ELTV, it became apparent that they were losing a nontrivial number of people who *did not* want to work over the holidays, and would quit. They were in demand, so it wasn't like they had a hard time finding another job. Then the agency would have to start over with the hiring and onboarding at the beginning of the year. I was later told that the ELTV framework changed the way that HR talked with finance, and finance could better see the reasoning behind some of HR's suggestions. HR could finally speak in a language that finance understood.

Be Careful

We want to stress again that you don't want to overargue ELTV. You don't say, "I've found a formula for any decision that you want to make in HR, and I built a spreadsheet to run it. Just plug in your information, and it will tell you exactly how much that benefit or change will be worth." That will not turn out well.

Instead, if there is not a shared worldview between the business and HR people, then this is a good way to get there. It's a good mental model for talking about how things relate—about how business and people are the same thing.

ELTV Template

It doesn't matter if you work on the HR side or the business side of the house—use this template or ask to see it, depending on your role. It lays out the information needed to have a meaningful discussion. The format and style of the template does not matter. What does matter is that the document covers four sections:

1. **Situation Analysis.** What's the current state of things? Use data and information from your company and supporting data from external studies.
2. **Proposed Solution.** How do you address the problem or leverage the opportunity?
3. **Return on Investment (ROI).** What is the required investment and the business impact?
4. **Obstacles, Challenges, and Open Questions.** No plan is free from obstacles. Be up front about what those are.

Putting the Template into Practice

Here's an example of a filled-out template.

Situation Analysis

We find that our employees are stressed out about their work-life balance, and it may be contributing to our turnover, which is 32 percent per year.

Looking at the ELTV curve, that means we have to replace those people, and each time that costs us $11K between finding them and ramping them up.

Our failure rate for new hires is currently running at about 15 percent. As a result, we're losing around $2.7 million a year in sales.

Proposed Solution

Host a series of Mexican food-themed events for our employees.

We'll call it "Taco Tuesday." They will happen on the first Tuesday of each month for a year.

We will run engagement surveys each quarter in order to gauge employee sentiment around the various initiatives we have, including Taco Tuesday.

We will also continue to measure turnover and will review exit interviews of employees, in order to determine whether our hypothesis of work-life balance was mentioned as a contributing factor. If we are making progress against that stress, we hope to see that factor mentioned less in exit interviews.

Return on Investment (ROI)

We project that we'll need to buy 12,000 tacos, plus decorations and related material, at a cost of $21,000 for these events.

The investment could potentially be less if during the course of our monitoring, as described above, we find that employees seem uninterested in this benefit. If that is the case, then we will not need to pay for a full year's worth of Taco Tuesdays.

We expect employee turnover not to be eliminated but to drop such that we can reduce the $2.7 million we're losing (see Situation Analysis) to $1.7 million, meaning we'll have an extra $1 million in sales annually.

If three or more people out of the 50-person sales team end up staying for three extra months, we'll realize a positive ROI.

Obstacles, Challenges, and Open Questions

We are sensitive to any potential claim of "cultural appropriation." Therefore, if this experiment is approved, we will work closely with our Latinx employees in order to ensure that the events are perceived in the most positive light.

Of course, it's difficult to determine cause and effect. Our employees are not lab rats where we could measure the isolated effect of taco consumption. Therefore, you have to use some judgment. In aggregate, the things we're implementing should be reducing turnover. If we're making all the measurements we discussed earlier about cost to fill roles, onboarding time, productivity, retention, and so on, then we'll have a way to quantify our overall performance against these variables.

The engagement survey mentioned above can provide another set of data points. We are able to ask lots of questions about how people feel about working at the company, what the most important and least important benefits are in their opinion, what have been highlights, and their suggestions for changes going forward. It's not hard data the way retention rates are, but it can be a leading indicator and may help to guide the periodic discussion about which of our initiatives seem to be positive, negative, or inconclusive with respect to ELTV.

Imagine if HR evaluates all existing and proposed people practices using the ELTV framework. Certainly, there still will be many lively and even heated conversations about the best allocation of resources. But at least one thing will have changed: It will be the equivalent of two people who did not speak the same language suddenly being able to use a tool like Google Translate to break through the language barrier. It will take the relationship to a whole new and better level.

Notes

1. Organizations with a strong onboarding process improve new hire retention by 82% and productivity by over 70%. (Brandon Hall, "The True Cost of a Bad Hire," 2015).
2. https://www.bcg.com/publications/2012/people-management-human-resources-leadership-from-capability-to-profitability.

Chapter 3: Takeaways

Employee Lifetime Value (ELTV) is a framework for understanding the value associated with hiring and talent throughout an employee's entire time at your organization.

It can be represented by a curve with milestones for when the role was opened, when the employee was fully onboarded, the point at which the employee decides to leave, and their last day.

The true value of great talent is often vast, and the costs of getting it wrong are severe. Luckily, there are a number of things that any leader can do to help bend the curve in your favor.

If your goal is to **shorten the time that it takes to find and onboard a person to full productivity,** then focus on better sourcing, a more effective hiring process, and better onboarding.

If instead your goal is to **maximize productivity,** then your focus should be on finding more productive people, improving management, and having people work on higher-yield activities

Finally, if your goal is to **increase the length of time someone is productive** in the organization, then the solution is to improve the organizational culture.

Use the ELTV Template to situate the business case for HR activities in business terms:

Situation Analysis. What's the current state of things? Use data and information from your company and supporting data from external studies.

Proposed Solution. How do you address the problem or leverage the opportunity?

Return on Investment (ROI). What is the required investment and the business impact? Describe this in terms of increased ELTV to showcase the value to the business.

Obstacles, Challenges, and Open Questions. No plan is free from obstacles. Be up front about what those are.

Expert Insights: Andres Traslavina

Andres is Senior Director, Global Executive Recruiting at Whole Foods Market. He describes his background:
I have some experience in being very customer-obsessed. Amazon and Whole Foods Market have that as one of their core leadership principles. I think there should not be a difference between treating your customers and your candidates with the same level of satisfaction. You should expect for them to feel the same experience as they go through a shopping experience or through a recruiting experience.

I did spend some time working at Disney. I learned that magic that you feel when you walk through the parks—that experience is contagious. If a company can lead with that, and it prompts candidates to rave about their experience, people will come to your company because of those sound bites.

How would you say your hiring approach stands out?
We look to interview fewer people but provide an amazing experience. So even if you don't get the job, you will tell seven or ten people over dinner, "Hey, I went to Whole Foods and this was my experience. I didn't even get the job but still, you should really apply."

Our process has three components:

1. Can you do the job?
2. Would you love to do this? You said you *could* do it, but would you love to do this?
3. Can we work together?

Through each of those components we have ways of making that experience unique. For example, when I talk to someone about why Whole Foods Market, I ask, "Are you looking for a job, a career, or your true calling?" Some responses that I hear indicate that they're aligned with the person looking to become a part of something bigger than themselves—aligned with our mission to nourish people on the planet. On the other hand, if people focus very much on compensation, promotions, and status, then maybe we won't have mutual alignment.

Didn't you have a story where you were interviewing a candidate and when they entered their hotel room, you had their favorite music playing?

We borrowed the idea from Joie de Vivre, a boutique hotel chain that does that. We ask questions about the candidate, and one of them is about their favorite music. When they walk into their hotel room, it is playing. We partner with "the Guild," a local hospitality start-up in Austin, to help us execute this concept. As you know, a lot of companies put together a show to try to impress a candidate. We're actually against that. We don't send a limousine to the airport; we tell people to take an Uber. I've picked up people directly at the airport in my car because I find that it's just a better experience to have a person connect with me and have them calm their nerves down a little bit. So, it's being authentic, genuine, and not going over the top.

How do you learn those personal preferences so that you can provide a customized experience?

Our leadership recruiting process takes about 60 days from the day when somebody applies to offering a role. I'm collecting information the whole time. If you work at it, you can put together a picture of someone from a combination of the résumé, application, and what you hear if you listen closely through casual conversations. Our recruiting coordinators are the folks in charge of helping to schedule flights and other tasks. They also are trained to note down details of the candidate.

So, when we are arranging a leadership visit, the candidate will fill out a form. In it we'll ask in an appropriate way about some little things that for them are maybe irrelevant but are meaningful for us. That's the basis for us to be able to create that experience.

Many leaders care that people interviewing at their company have a good experience, but maybe not that they have a great one. Do you have any stories to tell about how you've actually built motivation for doing more than what a hiring manager might have traditionally done at a company?

I think it's a business case that is built over time. What I can tell you, though, is not everyone is wired to create these great experiences. And I agree with you—good and great are different. We are very careful when hiring people in our recruiting teams who are wired to provide that amazing service, and who enjoy going to that level of greatness. Some of our coordinators have been so successful at this that sometimes I have to stop them because they want to do so much. They came from a wide variety of industries including education, hospitality, and customer-based retailers. You can teach recruiting and how to source, but you cannot teach how to provide an amazing experience, or how to smile in a genuine way.

Have you found that you need to do things in the candidate experience differently to make that experience more inclusive?

Yes, starting with not looking at the traditional data points to include someone within a process. We don't require degrees, and buzzwords don't mean anything. Our processes are set up to hire the best person. By default, when you have a process that focuses on hiring the best, you will hire a more diverse workforce. Do we have to improve it? Of course, we do. But I think the college-degree thing is a great example of focusing on things that may exclude people who could be great at the job. The attributes that make great leaders at Whole Foods are generosity, appreciation, love, emotional intelligence, purpose, resilience, servant leadership, being self-aware, and having integrity. Those cannot be taught; you either have them or you don't. Everything else can be taught.

How do you screen for people who are wired in the way that you want them to be, for those traits that you can't teach?

If I tell you, I'll have to charge you a lot! I mean, that's a million-dollar question. Look, it is really hard. It is because what you're trying to do is to look for what's underneath the surface. We can see knowledge and competency, but it's harder to see adaptability, positivity, and resilience. The best way to do it is by having a really good scientific structured questionnaire that studies your current top performers. And you extrapolate questions that you can ask your candidates and if they answer in a similar way, then they may be similar to your top performers. On a scale of one to ten with ten being high, how positive are you? After you conduct a study, maybe you will find that people who say eight are the ones who are like your top performers.

I don't think there is a company out there that has it figured out in terms of a scientific process. But fortunately, I have spent some time in the assessment world. I've tried to apply some of that in the way that we ask questions, so we can capture and understand people's emotional DNA as it relates to the things that are important to us.

Haven't you put something into place at Whole Foods Market that begins to create a thread that starts at hiring, and goes all the way through to talent performance management and employee experience?

Yes. We call it the Team Member Lifecycle where even when the employee or team member leaves the company, we want them to be an advocate and a fan. We want them to be great where they end up, and always be speaking positively about the company. Here are the areas of focus, and how we want people to think about us:

Attract. "I know what Whole Foods stands for and I want to be part of it."

Hire and Onboard. "I feel welcomed and supported right from the start."

Engage and Reward. "I feel valued and motivated to achieve my very best."

Serve. "I am part of something bigger and get to serve a higher purpose."

Perform and Grow. "I have opportunities to stretch and reach my fullest potential."

Exit. "I loved my experience, and I'm exploring what's next."

I could go on and on, but the idea here is to create genuine checkpoints with employees before, during, and after their time at Whole Foods Market, and continue to listen to them and engage with them. It pays big dividends.

4

Structured Hiring

Four words are at the heart of everything we discuss in this book. Two of those words—Talent Makers—are the subject of Chapter 9. The other two words are Structured Hiring. These simple ideas, when implemented consistently, can transform your organization. Although this chapter is short, it introduces the concept of structured hiring, which permeates the rest of this book.

When leaders have a financial problem, they know it. Their bank balance is low. When an organization has a customer problem, they know it—customers shout at them and leave for the competition.

But when organizations have a hiring problem, often the symptoms are misplaced and the leaders misdiagnose it. They don't really have a vision of what could be better; they just think it's always been bad and that it's unlikely to change.

The first problem is that they look at HR as a back-office function—a cost center. As we saw in the last chapter, if HR does not speak the language of known costs *and known returns*, then it will be easily marginalized.

We have a situation where the businesspeople misdiagnose hiring issues as "Why can't HR get its act together?" instead of the true diagnosis: "We used to think our job was making [bolts, software, policy papers, whatever]. But our first job is to become excellent at hiring people." That's the surest route to delivering those outputs.

The misdiagnosis continues: HR catches heat and then thinks the solution to its people problems could be a better ATS, as we discussed earlier: "If only my Applicant Tracking System (ATS) had a robust reporting engine, I could get my CEO that report that shows every single interview that was conducted this week—that's what we need." Or "If only an ATS had more buttons so the head of engineering could review 100 résumés for one position, then the problem would be solved."

What we found again and again is that organizations came to us with what they thought were ATS problems, and soon they realized that they instead had business problems.

Take diversity, equity, and inclusion (DE&I), for example. Some people come to us and say, "We have a problem with diversity hiring. We're looking for more female engineers. What can your ATS do to help us with this top-of-funnel issue?"

When we hear this, often what we'll find after further discussion is that the company *may* have a top-of-funnel issue, but *definitely does* have a candidate experience issue, as well as a problem with poor decision-making. The kind of candidates they want to hire are most likely getting sidelined in the loose, semi-process they're using that allows too much flaky decision-making. They often have an operational issue as well, because they don't have the data to know what is going on throughout the hiring process. They just know that they're not meeting their objectives.

The Master Plan

The first step to becoming world-class at hiring is what you're doing at this very moment—reading this book. The second step sounds so obvious:

Have a plan and follow it.

Everybody knows that, right? Common sense, right? Then why were we seeing company after company with no plan?

Somebody needs a job filled, so the job description gets posted on a website. After a while, people apply and then you start to do interviews. After the interviews, people discuss the candidates one by one: "I just met Rajesh. He seemed really good. What should we do next?" Someone says, "Let's interview him again." Meanwhile, your colleague interviewed Rachel and asked very different questions of her than were asked of Rajesh.

If you ask someone who's involved in this hire, "Where are we with filling this role? What's the next step?" the answer most likely will be "I don't know."

This halting, unstructured approach would have been laughable back in 1908 when the Model T was being assembled. No one would say, "So what do we do next? Maybe we should pick up some bolts and see where they fit?"

Therefore, when organizations come to us with what they think are ATS problems, our first order of business is to convince them that they need something that was a known concept more than a century ago: a prearranged plan. And it has to be written down to the real details of what their hiring process is. Then you follow that plan.

So What's in a "Good Plan"?

After we say that they need to create and follow a plan, we quickly have to get even more specific. That's because we hear:

"Oh, we have a plan."

"Good! Describe it to us."

"HR finds applicants, we interview them, and then we pick somebody."

Well, that is sort of a proto-plan. We have something much more detailed in mind. Over time, we've developed and refined the following characteristics of an effective plan that we call Structured Hiring:

The ideal candidate is defined by the business objectives of the job. This happens when the recruiter and hiring manager work together and get specific.

You use a deliberate and consistent process to evaluate all candidates. No more wondering where you are, and what's next. The process moves right along.

Your hiring decisions are based on data and evidence. Not only does this help to eliminate unconscious bias, but it also speeds up the process and results in better offers and better hires.

You learn and iterate. It's an upward spiral, where you can consistently get better at hiring, and distance yourself from your competition.

In the next four chapters, we will get highly detailed about the four competencies we introduced you to in Chapter 2. We'll see not only how they fit together, but also how they combine to deliver on having that detailed plan and effectively executing it.

Chapter 4: Takeaways

Structured Hiring is one of the foundational concepts in this book. It's about bringing a well thought-out, systematic rigor to the process of hiring.

Here are the elements of an effective structured hiring plan:

1. The ideal candidate is defined by the business objectives of the job.
2. Use a deliberate and consistent process to evaluate all candidates.
3. Your hiring decisions are based on data and evidence.
4. Learn and iterate.

Expert Insights: Jan Fiegel

Jan is Head of Talent at Sidewalk Labs, an Alphabet-owned company that's focused on urban innovation. Before joining Sidewalk, Jan built the recruiting function at Oscar Insurance, with hundreds of hires during his tenure. He has recruited for growth companies in Germany and the United Kingdom before coming to NYC in 2014.

What are some of the things that you need to navigate with leaders when you're making the case for structured interviewing?

I often get a chance to talk to CEOs, founders, and entrepreneurs, and here's what I say. Good recruiting is not harder than any of the other things you're doing: building a product, cultivating a team, or raising money from investors. It's not harder than that. But it's also not easier.

Another way to put it is this: Recruiting well requires the same rigor as an investor meeting. You would not go to meet an investor without having an objective and an agenda for that conversation, without having distilled your message, or without having researched the folks you will meet.

You would skip none of those things when it comes to most key business activities, but somehow we still operate with this notion that when it comes to evaluating a candidate in an interview, "I know it when I see it" is enough.

It is very clear from decades of research that we're all hardwired not to be objective. To counter that, I think about how to make rigor and intentionality easy. You can do this in the simplest of things—for example, with a template for how interview notes get written. When starting to write up summary notes, do not start with the conclusion; instead; write up the pluses and minuses first. I have learned that if I do it the other way around, I'll end up fitting the pluses and minuses to what my finished conclusion said.

When you look at organizations that do not have structured hiring, their process is typically messy and their decisions idiosyncratic, often driven by the loudest or most senior voice in the room. Compare that to a place where you have implemented structured interviewing, where rigor and intentionality drive the process and decisions, making it a better experience for everyone and driving better outcomes.

You have a different view of job descriptions. Could you describe it?

We need a whole different approach to job descriptions. Let's stop writing job descriptions in terms of responsibilities and let's start writing them in terms of outcomes. The reason is simple: Responsibilities don't drive success, outcomes do. You cannot measure my performance at the end of the year based on "Jan was responsible for the recruiting function."

When we know the work that needs to get done inside the organization, it can be helpful to carve it up by responsibilities: "You are responsible for this, I'm responsible for that." But it's a very poor measure of performance. It's also incredibly vague for candidates. By the way, this is not my insight; it's Lou Adler's, who has written on this extensively.

When you're defining a job, start with the outcomes you care about. We use Objectives and Key Results (OKRs). This centers your whole recruiting process on concrete, measurable deliverables. Then you assess the candidate's ability to deliver on those (versus making assumptions about which background best enables stepping into the responsibilities). Defining deliverables has the additional benefit of making it very clear to candidates what the work and the expectations of the role are.

Instead of saying, "In this role you are responsible for the recruiting function," I would say, "You're the Head of Talent and it is September. We need to hire 15 salespeople and another 10 engineers by the end of the year." That generates a very different conversation. And not least, when you make your hire, that person will come in with a clear understanding of what they need to get done; your performance management is already set up. You don't need to do more expectation setting—literally all you have to do is take the job description and say, "Well, how did we do against this?"

Once you define the job, please talk about how you interview for that.

The purpose of an interview is to predict success on the job, not just for the next month but preferably for the next few years. If we've defined success on the job by defining the deliverables, we can evaluate candidates against those. Next to past-oriented interviews, we use demonstration-focused formats like case studies, coding tests, or role plays to engage: "By the end of the year, you need to hire 15 salespeople and 10 engineers. What do you need to do?" And so again, focusing on deliverables creates a quick, easily translatable map around which to structure our assessment.

Hiring managers often just show up at an interview unprepared and ask about sports and schools. If you're really embracing structured interviewing, there's a whole bunch of prework that actually needs to be done by the hiring manager upfront, and that can feel onerous. Can you talk about how you've had success convincing hiring managers that they do need to put the work in at the front to be able to make better decisions and have better metrics at the end?

Ideally, we have an environment in which from the top down, it's clear that hiring is a priority. Still, sometimes you'll encounter an individual who hasn't bought in, for whatever reason. It's important to make it easy for them to do the right thing and frame recruiting through the business lens by giving them an analogy like the investor meeting example.

If I have a skeptical hiring manager, I may decide to do more of the work for them. It's probably going to look like "Hey, I drafted the scorecard for you. Let's talk about it," versus "Here's an empty template, go do it." So, it's a little bit about hand holding and making it easy for folks to succeed, until they see the results for themselves.

What if a leader says, "Okay, I want us to interview like this going forward, but changes need to happen on the recruiting team, too." How do you handle this?

I agree! Structured interviewing only works as a partnership. Now, one of the biggest reasons for underperformance of recruiting is under resourcing. I'll hear recruiters say that they handle 20+ requisitions at a time. You cannot drive best practice when you're overwhelmed with transactional duties.

When I speak with leaders, often they are willing to invest their own time; but I point out that they must also stand up a Talent function that actually has the bandwidth to do its job. Again, I come back to the model of running it like a business function: Match resourcing to the workload, then measure performance. You would not let your Head of Sales get away with having no sales capacity model, no process, and no script for how they will close X many accounts for the year.

Let's say you came into a new company, and the CEO was onboard with trying structured hiring. How would you answer this question: "Where do we start, in order to show results quickly?"

You have to start with a conversation about the nature of your hiring. By that I mean a few specific things: What volume of hires? How quickly? What functions—what's the work? Because if you're telling me, "Jan, next year, you need to hire 250 salespeople" that will be very different from "Jan, next year, we're gonna hire 150 engineers." That in turn is different from "Next year, we're growing the organization by 300 and it's going to be all unique roles across the board."

The easiest place to begin structured hiring is first to pick a role that you're hiring a lot, so that you can make a consistent plan, execute, train, and learn. It's much more difficult if you basically hire every role only once. The one-offs make it very hard to come up with a repeatable process where your teams calibrate, where you can tweak a process, get feedback, and see what works. Tilt the odds in your favor by choosing the right role to work on first.

Expert Insights: Gerardo Alvarez

Please give us a little background about what you do.

I work at Alphabet, the parent company of Google. I previously was part of a team called Mergers and Acquisitions—Technical Integrations. It focused on a variety of aspects of integrating acquired companies into Alphabet. I've also worked with most of the Alphabet companies on business system implementations, including HR and finance systems.

Could you describe the types of companies you work on at Alphabet?

Not counting Google, they range from companies that have started with just a handful of employees up to medium-sized businesses at the time that they became independent companies. They also range from being new to hiring, to having established practices around it. No matter the size, most of them have been in a pretty explosive growth phase.

How do you go about implementing a structured hiring approach within a new organization?

First, a structured approach definitely helps, because it creates consistency. When it's time to analyze data and find insights, you can actually find the data you need. If instead you have an ad hoc approach, where people just jump in and start doing things instead of thinking what should be in place, then it will be very difficult to gain insights. They end up spending their time cleaning up after themselves.

You need stakeholder agreement and systems discipline in order to implement structured hiring. Those companies that I've worked with that know what they want, are disciplined, and tend to have much better results. At first, they invest a lot of time to figure out what their processes should be. But eventually they get to a phase where they can take much deeper looks or insights at data and then make further process improvements in order to get the best talent. They are continuously reflecting on what's working, what's not working, and then fine-tuning things instead of making dramatic changes. The second order of business is to be focused on data and reporting, but the first order is to agree on processes and be disciplined.

How have you handled the recruiting ops function, where someone is thinking about what processes and systems to use, how to train people, and so on?

When companies are in early stages, they don't have a full-time recruiting ops person but it's typically someone on the recruiting team that fulfills the function. It's a critical function because in teams where there isn't someone like that, the wheels start falling off very quickly and it becomes a mess.

What are some of the recurring pain points that you've found in companies you've worked with?

One is that people tend to overthink some of the decisions in the hiring process. Some companies tend to have many more stages than they should, in order to arrive at a decision. That's a sign of decision paralysis. It often shows up when you have too many interviews. The solution is to make sure people specifically identify the areas that they should assess in a candidate. This makes the process more focused so that the candidate is assessed on the things that matter the most.

Another typical issue I've seen is not only having too many interviews and stages, which end up taking more time, but also introducing too many gates into the process. For example having a hiring committee stage in addition to individual decision makers. It's better to rethink the whole talent acquisition (TA) process and focus on the things that matter the most. That not only provides a much better experience for the candidate, but it gets to a faster conclusion about who is the best candidate. Otherwise, if you don't have a thought-out plan and don't know what good looks like, you just keep interviewing.

What are some of the ways you refine the hiring process over time at your companies?

A couple of things come to mind. First, after you've spent time defining what the processes should be, you need to have something that lets you know when things aren't conforming to the processes and rules that you defined. Sometimes, it takes a couple of dashboards that show you the exceptions. Then people can go and train those who didn't know what to do, or just didn't do it. It's really important that data hygiene is carried on over time. People tend to forget, or aren't as disciplined as they need to be. That's where the training comes in.

Second, something that's very useful is to look at who are good interviewers and good hires. In other words, when someone is hired and is successful, how did they do in the interview process? Who were their interviewers? Who were their hiring managers? Try to identify the patterns of what is working and not working. It takes a little bit of diligence to close that feedback loop, but it's worth it. You cannot think of recruiting or talent acquisition as a separate function that's only up front in the funnel. It's something that has to be part of the whole people landscape. You have to look at it holistically, from the perspective of the entire time that someone works for a company, and not just during the recruiting phase.

5

Own Every Moment of Your Hiring Experience

We've established that the traditional view of HR and hiring as an administrative function is narrow and seriously flawed. It effectively throttles what is potentially the most powerful engine in your organization, and that is the ability to hire great people.

There's another view that's mistakenly narrow. It's that the candidate experience primarily involves the job application on a website. Although it does involve that, it's so much more, and it deserves your close attention.

In order to become great at the hiring experience, you first have to define its wider boundaries. The experience starts when people become aware that your organization exists—in other words, your brand. Then they apply for a job, and hear (or don't hear) the results. Then hopefully they get an interview, then an offer, and they accept.

But it does not stop there. We consider the candidate experience to go beyond acceptance to their first day on the job, and then through onboarding—that critical first 30 days or so, when a decision to join is either validated or doubt is seeded. There are easily several dozen touch points in the candidate experience, whether organizations realize it or not and engineer those touch points or not. That means dozens of opportunities to impress or to drop the ball and pay for it with your reputation and hiring ability. This chapter is about making those experiences as good as possible, both for candidates and for the people involved in hiring them.

Top Talent

We assume that you're not reading this book so you can become "sort of okay" at hiring. You want to become head-and-shoulders-above-the-rest great at hiring, correct? If the answer is yes, then that means you are pursuing talent that is also superior.

Here's the problem with that great talent: It's much more in demand than other talent. These people are almost the opposite of average talent. Let's assume for a moment that a run-of-the-mill decent candidate needs to apply to 10 jobs in order to get an offer from at least one of them. The most sought-after candidates may get 5 or 10 offers and decide to take one. They can choose to work for any organization in their field, anywhere in the world, at any time.

You may decide that you want to roll out the red carpet for this special talent, but that's no longer possible. In the days when companies controlled what information was released about them, the red-carpet treatment may have worked. But now in the time it takes to eat a ham sandwich, the talented person can get a full data dump about you from Glassdoor, and corroborate that information with other social media, plus connections garnered from LinkedIn.

You're no longer in control—at least not in the way that your predecessors were in the good old days. Now the only way you can be in control of your reputation is to think about the hiring experience and make it so good that perfect strangers will interview with you and write you glowing reviews, *even if they don't get the job*. If you become that good, then yes, you'll be able to attract amazing talent at will.

"But the numbers prove I'm in the driver's seat, because I always have many more candidates than I have openings."

Let's look at those numbers. When you talk about hiring, you're mostly talking about people you're *not* hiring. In other words, you have 45 job applicants and you choose one, leaving 44 people who can—and a few percent of them will—light you up on social media and on Glassdoor. All these places are informing the decision of that next star candidate you so badly desire.

In an interview, these top candidates are looking you over with a critical eye the same way you're looking them over. You scrape up as many dollars as you can from everywhere and plop it before the star candidate—your great offer. What they know and you do not is that another organization with a lot more money and fame than you have decided to slide across a piece of paper with an eye-opening number on it.

Okay, so you lost that one. But let it be a lesson to you to focus relentlessly on the candidate experience and on your hiring brand, as rated by people over whom you have only the control that comes when you impress them from all angles.

What Are You Posting?

Many organizations do not make a clear distinction between three documents: The job description is the internal document that outlines the responsibilities, requirements, expectations, pay, and so forth; the job post lists the open role on an organization's website, with enough information and enticement to appeal to talented people so they decide to submit their information; and a job ad is a placement on an external site like Indeed.com or ZipRecruiter, meant to get people to click through. They often do not take the time to customize these documents to fit the audience.

The first problem is with the content of the posting. It's usually paragraph after paragraph of dense, bullet-point language and meaningless jargon. Trash, really. Many of the requirements range from unnecessary to absurd. We've seen examples where the number of years of required experience is longer than the technology has been in existence—for example, relating to Bitcoin.

We think someone who has great information about rewriting job posts is Katrina Kibben from Three Ears Media.[1] She has lots of useful advice on the topic. Here are a few of her points:

- Most job posts do a poor job with the job title, yet that's exactly the field that is searched by just about everyone. Because there are no industry standards around job titles, it's worth aligning the title with the most searched-for variations of that job. There may be a huge difference in results if you title a job "Data Scientist" versus "Data Analyst." Do some Google Trends searches and see if one variation is much more popular than the rest.
- Don't just mention a skill like "Java." Instead, translate the skill into everyday activities that the job will involve. Describe what they'll be using Java to create. Even include sentences that start with "After one year, you'll know you were successful if … ".
- See where you can shorten the job post; 200 words is a good length to shoot for. Stick to what is essential for the candidate to do the job, and don't put in a lot of stuff if you're not sure what is important.

The second problem is that the job description—if done well—has a purpose inside the organization, but what potential applicants should see is a job post that reads more like an advertisement. It should be accurate but also compelling. The goal is to make the target competitive candidate sit up, take notice, and be convinced to apply.

The third issue is that almost no one customizes or split-tests these documents. If we hope to get an internal applicant for a job, then the post on the internal careers page should sound different, with perhaps some internal jargon or a different title. If the post will also be advertised on campuses or specialized boards, think about doing other versions of the same post but with language that's tailored to those narrower audiences.

Strategic organizations will split-test posts to see if particular headlines pull differently. They'll also test different descriptions to see if they attract different kinds of applicants.

What Are You Mapping?

A lot of organizations spend considerable time mapping out their customer journey. In fact, there is a whole conference circuit for people interested in learning the intricacies of customer journey mapping.

We're not aware of any conferences whatsoever on the topic of hiring experience mapping.

Quietly though, the best organizations at hiring are doing just that. In Chapter 2, we mentioned how Airbnb leaves welcome notes for candidates being interviewed. We suggest that you map all your interactions with people during the hiring process and see where you can similarly stand out. You should have little trouble enhancing your brand and thus distinguishing yourself from the competition.

Mutual Pain

If you ask most recruiters, "Tell me about the worst day in the history of your recruiting career," you are most likely to hear about an event they worked. It's not much better for the potential applicants either.

It's a combination of overload and poor technology. If you're the recruiter, you may have collected 200 résumés after spending hours on your feet. You then flop down in your hotel room, go through the résumés, and try to remember whom you liked and didn't like. Then you scramble to try to set up interviews the next day with the people you think you liked. You may even need to type their résumés into your system. Often, recruiters will know that they are successful at hiring people recently out of school, but they won't know if it was from the recruiting effort there or from receiving applications in other ways.

It's all a process that hasn't changed in decades. When we ask recruiters why they go to these campuses if they're not sure how many candidates they get, and how many have actually turned into hires, the answer is shockingly consistent: "We go to the campuses because one of the execs at our company went there and insists that we go."

If you're the potential applicant, it's not much better. For the most part you're either asked to enter your information manually, or you hand your résumé to the recruiter and probably hear nothing back.

If you recruit at such events, at the very least it will be important to take any manual process out of the applicants' side. If you're handed a résumé, then have an app (ours or someone else's) where you can scan in the résumé, and take notes. Even a smartphone scanner will be better than the manual process. Or you could ask them to email their résumé to you on the spot, and if possible, you can take a few notes about the person between conversations.

Multiple Cooks in this Kitchen

There's another way that you have less control than you may think you have. Your reputation is the sum total of not just your efforts, but also the efforts of multiple people throughout your organization.

Who wrote the emails that automatically get sent to applicants? We should back up: Have you ever seen the emails that go from your organization to applicants? If you have, because you wrote them, then maybe they're great. But it could be that someone with zero recruiting experience wrote those, and you may be surprised—not in the good sense of the word—to learn what they say. Those emails are one of the first impressions made on applicants.

Is the language dull and bureaucratic sounding, full of stuff like "Your application has been received and is being processed," as if they're a bag of bolts? Or does it make your brand proud? We don't mean to suggest that these emails should gush enthusiasm, only that your brand should be stronger and not weaker after someone reads your emails.

If this person has already applied for jobs at your company, does the email sound like the business has never met the applicant before?

Let's say things are moving to the next stage and you've contacted an applicant and invited them in for an interview. It's likely that you are personally doing none of that, but that someone with a title of coordinator or the equivalent is doing that work.

Pretty senior people in organizations are often surprised to realize that pretty junior people are responsible for multiple important touch points in the hiring experience. They are usually paid near the bottom of the scale, but will be scheduling interviews, and possibly getting on the phone with candidates if some details require it. They become the voice and brand of your organization.

Perhaps you have a great coordinator who's been effectively trained at making that good first impression, someone who is friendly and welcoming, and who has a good command of all the sorts of questions that might be asked at that stage. Perhaps you don't have such a person.

Do you know who does it? Have you checked what's being said? Does an FAQ-type document exist with the answers you want candidates to hear when they ask various general, beforehand questions about the interview and the organization?

Information Candidates Can Use

Conscientious candidates typically will be geared up for interviews and can get nervous about the prospect of how the interview will play out. What are you doing to distinguish your brand at this point? Here are some of the questions candidates want to know about the interview, and which you should provide via email before the interview:

If the interview is in person:

- What is the exact address?
- Where do I park?
- Will I be reimbursed for any expenses like a ride, parking, and the like?
- If there are multiple similar buildings and entrances, how do I get to the right one? (Send a photo of the door with a big arrow.)
- What should I wear?
- What should I bring?
- Who will be interviewing me?
- How long will it last and is there a hard stop at a certain time?
- In addition to meeting people, is there any other component, like testing?
- Where are the restrooms?
- If I may need some water or food for whatever reason, where do I find that?
- Before I show up, do you have the number for someone I can text if for some reason I need to? For example, if there's a traffic jam due to an accident, or I have to cancel at the last minute?

If the interview is remote:

- Will it be by audio only or video?
- What is the phone number for me to call if I don't want to use my computer audio?

- Who will be interviewing me?
- How long will it last and is there a hard stop at a certain time?
- In addition to meeting people, is there any other component, like testing?
- If it's a long series of conversations or tasks, roughly when will we have breaks?
- What is the number for someone I can text if for some reason my computer freezes or I'm bumped off the call?
- Where is the documentation for the remote tool we'll be using (whether it's Zoom, Skype, etc.)?
- Where is the link to make it easy to test audio and video. For example, Zoom has a test feature for doing just that at https://zoom.us/test.
- Will the session be recorded, and will I later have access to the recording?

Names Are Important

It's often an awkward moment for everyone if a candidate has a name that may be unusual for native English speakers to pronounce. Candidates want to fit in and have a smooth experience, and they may be unsure if they should correct the pronunciation when someone makes a mistake. On the other hand, interviewers don't want to mess up and don't necessarily want to create an awkward situation by dwelling on a name too much. Do they not use the name? Or guess at the right way to say it? Or just ask?

The way we handle this issue at Greenhouse is we ask candidates to record and send us a short audio clip where we hear them pronouncing their own name. Then everyone interviewing has the spelling and sound of the name, before the interview even starts. You don't need Greenhouse software to make this happen. Most smartphones can do voice memos and those can then be sent via email or text. We highly recommend that you add this to the information you send to candidates before an interview. It shows respect, and almost no one does it.

Meet and Greet

Of course, remote working makes things different, but if the interview is in person, make sure you internally choreograph some of the first impressions: Who will greet the candidate? Will it be a receptionist, the coordinator, hiring manager, or someone else? And how can you help that person make the best first impression?

Where will the interview happen, and is that the best place? Of the options available to you, which ones would impress, which would be neutral, and which may even detract from the interview experience?

Does someone leave the candidate alone in the room, or stay and chat until everyone shows up?

Speaking of showing up, what do we know about whether interviews start on time and who is late by how much, or is known to be a no-show? You don't improve what you don't measure.

Is the seating arrangement something that's pleasant and effective, or might it make the candidate uneasy? For example, it might feel like an inquisition to have a row of interviewers on one end of the table and the candidate way at the other end. It might also be awkward if the candidate must constantly swivel their head in order to make eye contact with people on the far right and left.

Does anyone offer the candidate a beverage?

From the organization's perspective, you bring someone in for three hours of interviews. But from the candidate's perspective, it's also a three-hour taste of what it's like to work here. Do you have a culture where people will say "Hi" in the elevator or cafeteria to someone wearing a visitor badge? What would your first impressions be at your office? The goal here is to be observant and intentional.

During the Interview

We'll get into the actual substance of the interview in Chapter 7. At the moment, we're focusing on the experience instead of the substance of questions.

Will the candidate look at the interviewers and others they meet today and feel like they belong here?

Does someone have an agenda written out (physically or online, depending on the interview) and is it reviewed at the beginning of the interview?

We talked in Chapter 1 about the wealth of insights that can come from recording interviews. If you listened to a recording of interviews, does someone interrupt the candidate regularly? Does everyone give the candidate the time to provide complete answers? Sure, some people go on way too long when they could give a succinct answer. In that case, is anyone trained in skillfully moving the conversation along so the questions get covered in the time allowed?

Do the interviewers give the candidate a chance to ask questions? Or is that relegated to the last minute or two, when people are packing up and the interview feels like it's already over?

Does someone let the candidate know what the next steps will be without first being asked?

Some organizations will give out swag like a T-shirt before or after an interview. Do you have something like this? If done well, it can feel like a nice gesture; almost like "You're part of our community."

After the Interview

It's a nice touch when candidates send thank-you notes after an interview. Why not send the candidates a thank-you note? How many candidates will have ever gotten such a note?

Someone described to the candidate in the interview a timeline for what happens next. What data do you have for whether, in fact, that timeline was reasonably accurate? Of course situations arise, but if on a regular basis there's a wide gap between expectations and reality, something should change. Either tell future candidates about the realistic timeline, or determine if there's a problem with delays and whether that problem can be fixed.

If it's been determined that you'll not be progressing with the candidate, then when do you break the news? As we said earlier, it's bad form to do so while the candidate is still leaving the building. (True story.) We recommend that you send that email at least one day later.

It's also very bad form to ghost candidates. That sometimes happens with good intentions: "I'll put this sticky note right over here next to the others, reminding me to send a 'sorry to inform you' note ... " and then the note gets lost in a sea of stickies. Get a better system, even if it's just a dedicated calendar in Gmail to remind someone to send the notes at the right time. This helps to take stress off recruiters, who don't need to be mentally carrying around these sorts of tasks.

Speaking of that note, do you know what it says? Is it anything better and warmer than "We regret to inform you" language? We may be on to other things by that point, but a rejection letter is a sensitive thing for recipients. It's not necessary to lie, but it's a nice touch to make it sound—if appropriate—that you enjoyed meeting them, were impressed by something, and you wish things had worked out differently.

If some candidates get a second round of interviews, then how is that news delivered? Preferably it's with some enthusiasm, and also it should come from someone whom the candidate met. It should feel like a step up from the strangers we were before the first interview.

Of course, depending on the nature of the second interview, there should be another set of instructions about what's different. It may explain, "You'll be meeting with [so and so], who was on business in Europe when you came in for your first interview. We'll also be in a different building. ... " Also explain if the topics will be significantly different, or if other interview elements will be added, like testing.

Important Information for the Asking

Once again, there's conventional thinking, and there's the kind of thinking that contributes to hiring excellence. If you ask conventional thinkers how they measure the candidate experience, they may say, "We look at Glassdoor." As you know, we think Glassdoor is vital for everyone to review. However, it is often the case that only a small percentage of all candidates will do a review on Glassdoor.

Forward-thinking companies gather further useful information through the use of a survey in addition to monitoring Glassdoor. We've found that around 20 percent of the surveys get filled out—a much higher response rate, giving us that much more data. And get this:

You should also survey the candidates who didn't get the job.

That may be shocking to some people, but by now you already know the reason why—there are so many more of them than there are candidates who are offered a job. Also, they can have valuable observations about the process they just went through.

Here's how we do it. We wait until candidates have left the process, whether that's because they weren't accepted, they were made an offer and declined, or they were hired. Our approach is to send it two weeks after the candidate left the process.

We have a five-point scale from "Strongly Disagree" to "Strongly Agree." Here are some of the statements we'll ask them to rate us on:

1. Overall, my interviewing experience was positive.
2. My interview(s) started on time.
3. The position was clearly explained to me.
4. The people who interviewed me were well-prepared and conducted the interviews skillfully.
5. The interviewers got an accurate sense of my strengths and weaknesses.
6. I was treated with courtesy and respect.
7. Overall, I found the interview process to be challenging.
8. Overall, I have a more positive impression of the company after having gone through their recruiting process.

We also give the ability to make a comment about any of the questions and responses, in addition to the opportunity to tell us if there's anything they wish the company had done differently.

When the surveys come in, we anonymize them, so no one can associate survey feedback to any specific candidate or job. The aggregate information and stats then go to senior people at the department level.

If you're interested in being in the group that operates at a Systematic or Strategic level (and if you're reading this book, you should be), then you will find this continuous flow of information to be vital as a basis for continuous improvement.

Onboarding

Many companies think of new hire onboarding as the logistics of getting people a desk and a computer. Yes it's that, but it should be a great deal more than that.

Onboarding should be about how a candidate becomes part of the community as an employee. It should be how they learn the real culture and philosophy of the company. During the interview phase, we may have established *that* a candidate will be able to do a particular job. During the onboarding phase, we show that person *how* to do that job, and how to begin to navigate the company norms.

Of course, the coronavirus made this whole process that much harder. It used to be that you could sit near teammates or a designated buddy, and you'd learn a lot of the unwritten stuff by osmosis. That's just logistically harder when teams work remotely. Given how many organizations have said that they're not returning to the pre-2020 office arrangement and substantial numbers of employees will continue to work remotely, this onboarding challenge is with us to stay.

Just how important is it for us all to get onboarding right? Consider this:

- 20 percent of employee turnover happens in the first 45 days.[2]
- The cost to find and onboard a replacement is up to nine months of salary.
- 69 percent of employees are more likely to stay with a company for three or more years if they experienced great onboarding.

Let's look more closely at the current situation at most organizations.

The Big Void

The whole hiring experience—when it's successful for candidates—follows an upward trajectory from application to interview, then to the offer, and finally to a real or virtual handshake. It's pretty exciting stuff, especially for the candidate. On that day, the candidate savors how to break the news to friends and family. High fives all around! Then—nothing.

Organizations spend thousands of dollars to find and hire someone, and will spend tens of thousands or more to employ that person. They're expecting them to contribute tens or hundreds of thousands of dollars of value, or they wouldn't hire them. Yet they'll spend generously for ice cream for the new employee and will spend no time or money on onboarding.

It could be weeks between when someone accepts an offer and starts the job. So, this crescendo of hiring activity and positive emotions kind of cruises off a cliff into nothingness for a while. That is, until a short email arrives, telling you to show up on Tuesday at 9 a.m., and to bring your passport.

It's not necessarily a big surprise that this abrupt break happens: The recruiter's job is done, and the hiring manager is waiting for the employee to show up to work.

Meanwhile, in this vacuum, what's going through the candidate's mind? The afterglow from the good news begins to fade, and it's replaced by a simmering anxiety:

- Did I take the right job?
- What am I supposed to wear on the first day?
- Where do I go when I get there?
- Will I be able to find the bathroom near where I sit?
- Will people be nice?
- Am I going to be able to make a friend soon?

Nature abhors a vacuum, and in the vacuum created by no communication from the organization, their brain fills it with these anxiety-based thoughts. They don't sleep the night before the first day, and that just adds to their anxiety.

Avoid that Void

We've all been in the position of that candidate, so it's actually not that hard to predict the likely questions. Write them down and address them in different ways.

When it comes to highly specific questions about the job, the hiring manager can write an email or even deliver a short, personalized video to answer them. That takes care of all those details about where

I go, where I'll sit, who my buddy will be, and that we have a start class. This is a group of people who started at about the same time. In a large organization, there may be many start classes of a few dozen people each in any month, or it may be just one class each month. The hiring manager can indicate when and where the start class will get together.

Then for the larger questions about whether people will be nice, or what the culture is like, you could have an email or video from the buddy who should be identified before start day. Of course, its purpose is not to do some deep dive into the culture of the place; instead by simply having a friendly welcome message, most of the job is done. The buddy can explain briefly that they'll be sure to schedule some times to chat together and with other people, and how they're available from this moment on to answer questions.

Think about doing a short video from the CEO or department head. That video may not be customized to each particular person who's starting—but what if it was? Just imagine what the effect would be when the big boss takes the time to record a 30-second personalized welcome video to the new hire. How many people might the new hire show that video to? How proud will that person be, that the boss actually mentioned their name, something about how important the role is, and how they are looking forward to meeting them in the first week?

Create the Goals

Meanwhile, before the candidate even starts, the hiring manager should be thinking about what the 30-, 60-, and 90-day goals should be for that person. This is the place for the first concrete expression of how the new hire will figure into what's going on right now. The goals will naturally be very different for an engineer in New York versus a salesperson in the California office. It might not be delivered in detail ahead of time, but even so, the hiring manager can mention in an email that they've been thinking about appropriate goals at those milestone dates, and is looking forward to meeting and discussing them.

Behind the Scenes

Meanwhile, right after the person is hired, someone from HR should be in contact with the hiring manager so all the documents and details get transferred from the candidate's application to the forms that need to be filled out. Typically, it will be HR systems that need to talk with other systems, now that a new hire is involved. You may or may not have interfaces built to transfer that data. Preferably you do. Even if that's not the case, you can use the time gap between offer acceptance and first day to prepare documents with information you already know about the new hire.

Think what a better experience that will be on day one, compared to handing them a pile of forms that ask them to fill out their name, address, and so on, which makes it appear like we don't even know who they are. Let's fill all that known information out for them, so we telegraph that we were listening when they gave us all that information previously. It also means that we'll be getting that person past the paperwork and on to productive work that much faster.

You can think about the onboarding experience like a mini product launch. Who is involved in this person coming onboard? What can get done before the start day and not after? It may be that two weeks before that day, IT needs to contact the person with a welcome email, explaining what sort of systems they'll be tied into, and asking for certain information, so systems are up and running on day one. Then one week before start day, the hiring manager might write to voice enthusiasm once more at the person's joining the team. Perhaps there is also mention of a couple of meetings that are scheduled early on, relating to projects that are on the radar screen. Of course, the goal is not to load up the new employee with tasks and any sense of pressure. Instead, it's to telegraph that the person is valuable, part of a team, and we have a culture of great communication.

KPI for Onboarding

It's true that you don't improve what you don't measure. It's also true that you're unlikely to improve what no one is accountable for. We mentioned how during the hiring process it's necessary to have systems or people provide nudges from time to time, around filling in scorecards and such. It's a good idea to either have systems or a designated person monitor whether all these pre-start-day tasks are getting done, and indicate if they are not.

Think first about the metrics by which you can judge the success of onboarding. One of them could be when the hiring manager feels like the person is fully up and running. Yes, that's subjective, but important nevertheless. Another should definitely be the result of surveys you do of the new employee. After four days, you ask if they have all the physical materials they need to do their job. After 30 days, you ask, "Do you know what success looks like in your role?" After 90 days, you ask how the process has gone overall, and whether they are ready to start referring their friends to work here.

Review all the responses you get to identify issues, of course, but also do an analysis by start class, to see how you're trending.

You have the ability to transform onboarding from this blah bureaucratic function into an experience that will blow away new hires, and compel them to want to tell everyone about how they were given the red-carpet treatment by you. Add to that the efforts you make to improve the hiring experience in general, and not only are you likely to have increased Employee Lifetime Value (ELTV) for this person, but you may well have your newest, enthusiastic referral source.

Get Visible

Jon: On the first day of employment at Greenhouse, people walk in the building and get checked in. (Or they do the equivalent remotely.) The next thing they do is spend an hour with me, talking about Greenhouse, what we're all about, and why we're excited for them to be here. I get a ton of positive feedback from spending that one hour every so often. Occasionally, my peers at other companies will go, "You still do that?" Oh yes I do, because it's a super-leveraged use of my time. I can spend one hour, and it has the effect of setting a whole bunch of people off on the right foot, ready to do 2,000 hours of work each, in the coming year.

Daniel is just as involved as I am. He responds to comments on Glassdoor, each of us will occasionally personally interview senior candidates and make offers, and we have breakfasts and orientation sessions for new hires every two weeks.

Once you see the positive effects of leaders getting personally involved in the candidate experience, you'll scratch your head and not understand why more people don't take advantage of this very high ROI activity.

The Hiring Experience Is Not Just About Candidates

When we talk about the hiring experience, we're not only referring to applicants, candidates, and new hires. There's a whole other dimension, which is the experience that the rest of your employees have when they interact with recruiting. It's the internal experience.

That experience has a different feedback loop from the new-hire one, which tends to be about Glassdoor ratings. Let's say you ask the hiring manager to show up and participate in an interview. If that is an awful experience from the hiring manager's perspective, then one of three things will happen: They may not show up ("Hey, I'm sorry; we had an emergency."), or they'll be incredibly hard to book a time with, or they may show up and now do a poor job themselves. They might ask irrelevant, duplicative, or downright illegal questions, or be bored. That certainly will make it to the external ratings as well.

What are some of the issues that relate to the hiring manager?

1. **The process feels like a black hole, where no useful information escapes and makes it to the hiring manager.** They feel like they're forever chasing the recruiter. As extremely busy as recruiters are, they need to find even small amounts of time to play offense instead of only defense. One way is to give hiring managers good-looking, high-quality data and reports before being asked to.

   The hiring manager may feel like there is no forum to express what's needed in this role, and how the candidates are stacking up. This gets to the crucial step of having an effective kickoff meeting. We'll discuss this in Chapter 7. Also make sure the hiring manager is able to express what they think about this person versus that person. That may seem like an obvious requirement, but hiring managers sometimes feel left out when decisions get made about the candidate pool.

2. **Repetitive tasks are more cumbersome than necessary.** For example, if documents like job descriptions, résumés, and score-cards are stored in different places and have different filename conventions (or no standardization at all), then each of these touch points instead becomes a pain point for the hiring manager. Even if your systems are not highly automated, standard procedures can be put in place to make documents easier to find. Sometimes hiring managers are part of the problem by contributing to poor document practices. In that case, it's time to get together and come to some agreement about what the procedures should be, and how a lot of time will be saved and frustration avoided by taking these steps.

3. **Tools and processes don't adjust to different levels of hiring manager engagement.** Some hiring managers are more active and involved than others. Some are too active, and their "I'll do it myself" attitude can break systems. Don't have a one-size-fits-all approach. Ultimately, a lot of the recommendations in this book will result in a higher level of hiring manager involvement. In the meantime, it's best to adjust to each manager's comfort zone for tools. If some managers live in their mobile phones or in Slack, then do what you can to fit within their lifestyle. It will pay off.

If you are this kind of great service provider inside the organization, they're going to think: *Wow. Recruiting's really on its game. I need to make sure I step up and do my part, too. I don't want to be the one who slows things down.*

Notes

1. https://katrinakibben.com/2019/01/15/what-i-learned-job-postings/
2. https://bit.ly/3jzvU4Y

Chapter 5: Takeaways

The best people are in high demand. They have information, control, and many choices, so you must stand out.

Remember that mathematically, most applicants and candidates for your jobs will never get an offer from you, but many will not hesitate to describe the experience on Glassdoor and in social media. **You do not directly control your reputation;** candidates create your reputation based on the experiences they have with you.

Don't post your job description; it's for internal purposes. Instead, **create a job post that actually aims to attract great talent.**

Have you **mapped every impression and interaction** of your candidate experience? If not, you should.

As part of that experience, **create comprehensive, useful materials** to give candidates before they interview with you.

Systematically collect feedback from candidates about the process they went through, and have a system for reviewing and acting on that feedback.

New-hire onboarding is a **huge opportunity to make a powerful impression** on new hires, and to get them up to productive speed more quickly.

A great Structured Hiring experience also extends to interviewers, hiring managers, and other leaders. **Map those experiences** and work to make them easier and more effective.

Expert Insights: Jill Macri

Jill Macri led global recruiting at Airbnb. She was there for six years, from when it was around 100 people to about 4,000 people. She then co-founded a firm called Growth By Design Talent, which helps companies to navigate the high-growth experience when it comes to hiring.

What would you say are steps companies should take when they want to overhaul their candidate experience?

We work with two types of companies. One type has a really strong consumer brand, in which case they are overwhelmed with demand, with too many candidates coming into the top of the funnel. So, they have a filtration problem.

The other type of company effectively has no brand, so they're not getting any inbound interest. But with both, we start with the same fundamental question: What differentiates you? We work with a lot of tech companies, and they often lean on the same things—high growth, opportunity for impact, and so on—so candidates are hearing the same buzz words from every company. Giving a candidate swag during the interview process is not a meaningful differentiator.

We therefore suggest that companies first listen very closely to what candidates say about the process, based on surveys we do of both rejected and accepted candidates, and also through focus groups.

What are some misconceptions that companies typically have about the hiring process?

Every founder or leader will believe that the talent that they need to attract is unique. In addition—especially in the tech world—there is a certain arrogance around somebody winning the opportunity to come work for them. In that context, it sometimes comes as a surprise to companies that what they are offering candidates is actually pretty common, given the competitive environment.

At leadership meetings, we ask people to reflect on the last time they interviewed for a job and the different candidate experiences they had. That can be a real "aha" moment. They're like, "Oh, yeah, my interviewers were not even talking about the same job opening when they interviewed me," or "They took longer to get back to me than they said," and so on. They all can recall terrible experiences. I then ask them to really dive in and discover what the average candidate is getting at their company today. The candidate journey is the precursor to the employee journey: What messages about your values and culture are you telegraphing through your candidate experience?

What would you say are missed opportunities when companies are hiring?

The way we look at it, every candidate has a megaphone. The person you're interviewing may not be a customer directly, but perhaps at some point they will be the decision maker on whether or not a company uses your product. Or they'll have influence on the decision maker—their roommate is a great engineer whom you're trying to recruit. Every candidate becomes either an advocate for your brand or detractor of your brand.

You told us about a unique way you handled applicants whom you rejected at Airbnb. Can you describe that?

We had a survey for people who got rejected at the very beginning of the application phase. Many companies discount the experience of this candidate group, since they didn't make it past the online application. But we realized that from the applicants' perspective, they still had a candidate experience from the moment they applied and hit the "Send" button. We wanted to capture feedback there and be able to understand what could make that experience better.

What did you do in the way of surveys for new hires?

On Friday of an employee's first week, recruiting had an hour with them, where we talked about how to be a great brand ambassador for Airbnb, and what part they might take in recruiting. We also had them do a survey in the room, so that gave us a 100 percent completion rate.

The survey covered a lot, but one of the most important questions was what impacted your decision to join Airbnb? The other key question was at what point in the process did you decide you were going to join? That gave us really rich data to review. It basically told us the things that we were doing in the process that really made a difference.

For example, a part of our process was a values interview by a cross-functional team member with no skin in the game, just a conversation with somebody on values and culture. We found that the values portion of interviews were what candidates cited again and again as their reason for joining and it was the highlight of the interview process for them. This validated our investment in that particular interview.

Can you explain a bit about the Feedback Loop?

My firm worked with a different company of around 1,200 people, and did a candidate-experience design process with them. During the focus groups, we asked, "What was surprising once you joined? What do you wish you had known?" The majority of them said they didn't really understand what the company did before they joined. It was a pretty complex business, but even so, that was a surprising finding. They said that it was only around week three that they really understood the business accurately.

As a result, we suggested the marketing team put together an infographic. During the interview, the recruiter would take them through and really explain the business model and opportunities at each point.

Six months later, we did surveys of people who were new hires, and asked about the business model. Many people said that during the interview, the infographic was a huge "aha" moment for them about the business. We had basically pulled up the aha moment from week three of our *employee* experience to the conversation in the *candidate* experience.

If we look at the candidate experience, what would you say is something that readers of this book could immediately implement after reading it?

I am a huge fan of collecting data from surveys and focus groups. I also think that a lot of valuable insights can come from talking with new hires.

These people have just been through your process. They are by definition the very people you are currently trying to hire, and they also have most likely just been through experiences at other companies they were interviewing at. I regard these people as a very rich data source. For leaders, I find that this information is the most powerful, because if you do anonymous candidate surveys, people can kind of discount it as "Well, we might not have really wanted to hire those people anyway." But if you do it with a group of people whom they already value, it can be more meaningful.

Another useful thing was something we did in the days before COVID-19. In the cafeteria, we posted a timeline of the candidate process of application, recruiter screen, first interview, and so on. We had two colors of sticky notes next to the timeline. We just asked people to put up highs and lows in the process and stick a green or red note at the relevant spots. Over the course of a week, we got a whole lot of insights about what were the consistent lows and highs of the process. That gave us a basis to go back, iterate, and improve.

6

Attract the Best Talent

As advanced as our society seems to be, some things haven't changed much. Although newspapers aren't what they once were, and people do not buy want ads in newspapers, they're still doing the twenty-first-century equivalent: They place ads on Indeed, or LinkedIn, or ZipRecruiter and think, *There. We took care of that task.*

If all you do is take those simple actions, you're not really an active participant in the marketplace. You're a filter feeder, like some high-tech clam. You mostly sit there and applicants stream by, after applying at your website or through one of those mega sites. Similarly, your recruiter may have an idea in their head of how they do it. Why do they post ads on a certain job board this quarter? It's mostly because it's a familiar strategy. That could be one rung up from chaos.

We want to be clear that there is nothing wrong with quickly placing several ads for a role; in fact, we do it too. It's just that you can't stop there, because the competitive bar for attracting great candidates is now so very high.

You don't want to just hire the best of who happened to appear this week—you want to hire one of the best people *in the world* for this job. And how do you know who that person is? Well, there are about 700 million résumés on LinkedIn. You *could* look at all of them, but nobody has the time to do that. What's the alternative in order to

111

actually find the right person in the needed moment to fill that job? That's the capability we're talking about here.

Next Evolutionary Step from Filter Feeders: Recruiter Spam

Many recruiters know that filter feeding is not going to cut it, so they get active. The problem is how they get active.

They're sitting at their computer: *Okay, I gotta go find engineers.* They set a few filters on LinkedIn or another search engine, and then send their generic email blast to 100 engineers—with potentially irrelevant experience:

> Dear [First name],
> Acme Corp is looking for engineers and YOU SEEM GREAT. We are doing all kinds of challenging, interesting projects. We're a great company. We've got free Ping-Pong. You should totally apply. ...

The recruiter sits back in satisfaction. *Cool, I did my sourcing for the week.*

As we mentioned in Chapter 1, recruiters will do the same thing with dedicated candidate pools like meetups. One of them will stumble on this vein of high-grade engineer or designer ore, and raise their fists above the computer in triumph: a source that seems untouched by other recruiters! And it very well might be. However, the recruiter takes out their one trusty, useless tool and straightens up at the keyboard:

> Dear Jose,
> I came across your profile at the New Hampshire Print Designers' Meetup. ...

That experience is very different from the point of view of Jose, the recipient of that email. He gets variations of that email 30 times a day and ignores all of them like they're just noise. It was a pure waste of time to send them.

Let's think about the people whom you want to work at your company. What's their perspective on your company? Most of them have never heard of you, never mind know that they should work there. Most of these great people aren't even looking for jobs right now. It's a matching problem where the matches are just really sparse. You've got 8 billion people in the world, 10 million organizations, and you're one of them. How do you effectively connect?

The recruiter thinks, *That's why I sent the email! Now they know about me.*

How's that working for you?

You've got this little squirt gun, and you think you're an army.

Filter feeding doesn't get the job done, nor does push-button spamming. You need to become an active participant in this marketplace. You must make a lot of choreographed moves in multiple areas. It's going to require a lot of time, effort, brainpower, and machinery in place to make sure that you're really good at connecting with the right people.

Great hiring has become more like great marketing. In the past, we were able to market by putting up a billboard or newspaper ad, and maybe some customers would respond. Our recruiter/spammer is stuck in that past. Now what you have to do with great marketing—or great hiring—is move from something that feels very general and ad hoc to something personal, systematic, and measurable. There may still be an element of chance that the very best candidate sees your job opening, but in this case, Thomas Jefferson's concept is still true: "I am a great believer in luck, and I find the harder I work, the more I have of it."[1]

Once-and-Done Talent Sourcing Is a Thing of the Past

Organizations that want to be great at hiring must adapt to another seismic shift in the marketplace. It used to be that careers were really long. Daniel's dad had one job his whole life, and then he retired. That wasn't unusual because for many jobs, you could hire someone and then that job was effectively filled forever. Forty years later, you gave them a pension, a party, and a gold watch. That slot then opened up for someone else.

Now at any given moment a good amount of that talent is flowing away to other opportunities. Even if you're not a hyper-growth company, you're hiring people much more frequently than you were a generation ago.

That's not necessarily a reflection on your company: Even if you have created a great work environment, you'll have good talent leaving your company. Look no further than PayPal, for example, where former employees and founders went on to create Tesla, YouTube, and LinkedIn, among many others.[2]

As a result, you've got to create the conditions where you can have a steady flow of great talent coming into your company. It's the only antidote to great talent leaving.

> *Jon:* We had this very situation not long ago in our Customer Success (CS) organization. We had hired some really good people there. In the space of two months, three of them became heads of CS at other companies.
>
> Some of the team were like, "Oh my God, what's happening? We can't keep anyone!" I had to calm them down: "Hey, that's the point! We're hiring great people, they stay here a while, and then they become leaders at other companies. As much of a bummer as it is for us to lose those people, it's great for them. It's a positive that we're putting advocates everywhere—it's what we want for you."
>
> It creates an opportunity for us to go hire somebody else who's amazing. And by the way, what's my pitch to that next person I'm going to hire? "Why did the last person leave? They got a big pay raise and are now running CS down the street."

How did companies source people a generation ago? If you were in the white-collar sector, you went to top universities and hired graduates; otherwise, you took out ads in the paper. Either way, you had a narrow set of sources, found people there, and hired some of them.

That's no longer our world. That machinery people built at companies to go a few places, do your thing, and then be done— that's not the right machinery anymore.

Real Competition

It's not just that candidates have all sorts of choices today. It's that while you're working your one or two semi-passive sourcing methods, many other companies out there are working their asses off and lavishing these people with attention and effective, very targeted messages.

They're getting to know potential candidates. They're inviting them to speak at their meetup and have pizza with them. They're identifying which of their friends may have some meaningful connection with the candidates and having their friends write. Companies take out national television ads during NFL football on how it's such a great place to work for software engineers. And you're sending a canned message?

It's also a highly dynamic market with methods whose effectiveness decays in a couple of years, or maybe just in months.

> *Daniel:* I was one of the first half million members on LinkedIn, joining in 2005. I was a working programmer, so I could send a message to another working programmer on LinkedIn and say, "Hey, I see you're also into dot net. Want to get some coffee?" I usually heard back something like, "Sure. When looks good for you?" Just being on LinkedIn together was enough of a connection. Now even if I'm not a recruiter but a peer, that doesn't work anymore. Just too much spam.

As a result, you have to be alert to the constant change, and adapt your methods to be highly personalized and proactive. It's a worldwide ocean of organizations and talent, and you're one little participant in it. Do you want to be a shark, or a clam?

The Pressure's On

We just talked about how recruiters need to step up their game if they have any hope of connecting in this much larger, more jaded, and more competitive marketplace. At the same time, they're continuously being pressured from the business side with emotion-laden variations of "What do you have for me for that Northeast SDR position?"

Before we get into more detail about specific sourcing options for expanding the candidate flow, it's important to first discuss how you measure success. How good or bad are we doing with attracting candidates in general?" That's the question that leaders must regularly ask.

It can be answered with overall statistics about how many openings we have to fill right now, how many were filled in the last 30 days, and so on. But that's just the output. We need to know how the machine is working in detail. This chapter is about creating the environment where the deeper question can be answered with the confidence that comes from a comprehensive and effective sourcing strategy.

Let's all admit something right up front: Even when the machine is working smoothly, it's really challenging to get reliable, granular data on how well you're doing with specific techniques; never mind what you should specifically do in order to get better. Why is that?

First, let's consider data tracking. It's messy because some applicants come in from what you have on your site; you went out and found others at events; still others clicked on a job board; some were internal applicants; and some looked like they came in cold but were actually the result of a referral by a current or former employee.

Next, the way you judge the success of finding people varies greatly, depending on the job. If you're trying to go after data scientists in New York City, there are literally more jobs than there are candidates to fill them. It's an entirely different situation when you want to fill an entry-level SDR role in New York City. That's a candidate-rich environment, where you can open a job and get dozens of applicants by the time you're back from lunch.

It's also a challenge to find reliable benchmark data for your industry in order to gauge your success against something external. Even if you do have some benchmarks, success can be judged on several different levels:

- How many candidates applied?
- What was the diversity of those candidates?
- How fast were you able to generate them?
- What did you spend to get them?
- How comprehensive a sourcing plan did you have to create and follow in order to get them?

In the context of how busy recruiters are—and how difficult it is to measure success of the component parts—most organizations default to doing more of what they've done all along. Their standard way of doing things has become their path of least resistance. It's like the person we mentioned in Chapter 3 whose sourcing plan was to hit a built-in button in the Applicant Tracking System (ATS), which posted the position on a job board.

Who Decides What

There is a lot more outside of a recruiter's control than there is within it. Typically, it's the head of recruiting who makes big-picture, annual decisions about how candidates will be sourced: We're going to buy 10 licenses of LinkedIn Recruiter; we will renew our annual license on Indeed.com; we'll adjust our referral program so this year we'll give out $3,000 for every referred person who gets hired; we have a new initiative this year for an internal mobility program, which will encourage employees to think about moving to a different unit in the organization; and so on.

Then at the specific job level, when you open up the job, many things happen more or less automatically: The job gets posted on the website, and a certain number of people come in that way. You see a few referrals and Indeed.com picks up the post, so applications come in that way. This background level of activity pretty much happens without much involvement by recruiters.

If you set aside the two groups of activities we just listed, that leaves us with what's within the recruiter's control. They can certainly go to LinkedIn and send out emails. They can make the case for spending agency dollars on this job, though it better be a pretty strong case, given how expensive agencies are compared to standard budgets. It may be easier to make the case to spend job-board dollars, but that's limited, too. What we usually see is that the recruiter's variable response to different job needs mostly revolves around how many outbound emails they send to strangers. The good news is that there are many more activities that can be within the recruiter's control, as we'll see.

The Elements of Successful Candidate Attraction

We've said that some organizations get different and better outcomes because they think and act differently. When it comes to sourcing candidates, three key perspectives are necessary:

1. **You must take a portfolio approach.** There is no single answer to sourcing, no single job board or other avenue.
2. **Each technique can be optimized and improved.** There's no on/off switch where you turn on campus recruiting, for example. The endlessly changing marketplace means the only truly effective approach is to be continuously improving those techniques.
3. **Trying harder does indeed work better.** Yes, occasionally it's possible to "try smarter", but by and large, the people who lean into the work and put in serious efforts are going to be the ones who get out-sized results.

Daniel: In my experience, most companies and people really don't have a sense of what the possibilities are. I was talking to someone who said, "Man, it's really hard out there to find engineers. We've tried everything."

"Wow. Really? So what have you tried?"

"Well, I placed an ad on Craigslist. And I hired a recruiter that I used in my last job. Nothing has come of this. We're screwed."

I'm like, "Wait. You've. That's all you've done? You have not even started!"

People not only have a lack of awareness of the broad range of things that companies can do to get candidates, but they aren't properly calibrated in terms of how much to do. They may do one post on Indeed.com or three emails on LinkedIn. When I sit with them, I explain, "Okay, in the next hour, we're going to send 80 highly personalized outreach emails. Let's go."

Optimizing a Portfolio

Let's stick with the concept of reviewing a portfolio of techniques for finding candidates. Like any portfolio, you have a variety of things with different characteristics, which means you can mix and match to try to accomplish your objectives. Figure 6.1 lays out a framework for thinking about how different hiring goals map to various techniques available to you.

Any sourcing technique can be evaluated along four main characteristics. Some are great at one or two of these characteristics, and not

Optimize for	Variety of techniques for sourcing
Cost	Job board advertising
Speed	
Effort	Career site
Diversity	Referrals
	Agency
	Sourcing software
	Cold outreach outbound sourcing
	Sourcing from database
Analyze by role differences	Internal
Candidate-dense roles	Social media
Candidate-sparse roles	Events

Figure 6.1   How Different Goals and Jobs Require Different Sourcing Techniques.

so good at the others. When you have a particular hiring objective, these characteristics come into play and influence your decision. Let's go through each.

Cost. Staffing agencies are at the high end of the cost spectrum. They generally give you a really good quantity of candidates. They don't give you 100 candidates, or only two. They'll give you 10 to 15, which is great. The other thing staffing agencies will do is provide fairly prequalified people and not a random array by any means. The problem is you're looking at around $25,000 per job opening for all this convenience.

In the hiring world, there's a lot of negativity toward agencies for charging the fees they do, among other reasons. Why are they still around, then? Because agencies give you just the right quality and quantity, though it comes at a price. You are paying for convenient results.

There was a time when agencies were able to assemble proprietary sets of candidates. If you wanted to find these pockets of candidates with particular characteristics, you needed to go through them.

They had access to that part of the market and you did not. It was similar to the situation Daniel described in Chapter 1, where if he wanted to find lists of companies who might want to hire him, he had to buy a book.

For the most part, agencies no longer have strangleholds on information. They have the same Rolodex™ that you do of many hundreds of millions of names. It's called LinkedIn. They are not doing anything that you couldn't do. They have a process, and are willing to throw bodies at sending the emails and doing the work. It's when organizations either don't know how to source, or don't want to put in the effort, that they're willing to write out that fat check.

There is one exception to this, and that is highly focused agencies. Some of these have taken the time and done the legwork in really specialized niches. Therefore, if you're looking for a particular type of data scientist in a certain location—and you don't need such people very often—it can make a lot of sense to hire an agency whose wheelhouse is exactly that kind of talent.

Speed. Sometimes it can make a huge difference if you're able to fill a role in 10 days instead of in 60. Agencies often are the default solution when organizations need positions filled fast. However, if a company has taken the time to cultivate a robust referral program, then that approach can yield as good or better results, and at a much lower cost.

Effort. Some approaches require a lot of effort but can really pay off. For example, it takes considerable time to do deep targeting on LinkedIn, to send dozens or hundreds of emails to people there, and have one-on-one conversations. The same is true of attending meetups and getting to know the members. If that hard work is done in the vineyards over time, so to speak, then at some point you'll be able to turn to that channel and harvest the results.

Diversity. Different techniques will deliver varying levels of diversity when it comes to the candidates they produce. For example, it's common for people to know and refer candidates who are a lot like themselves. That can be great, but it may not help to meet your diversity, equity, and inclusion (DE&I) objectives in some cases. However, taking the time to cultivate pipelines on campuses or searching for specialized job boards could be ways to deliver very different pools of candidates to the top of your funnel.

Role Differences. As we said earlier, some roles are vastly more difficult to fill than others. If you have a challenging, candidate-sparse role, then you're going to throw every technique you have to get it filled. However, candidate-dense roles are much more forgiving; you may be able to fill those from just your own career site or database of previous candidates.

Variety of Techniques

Because we're writing this book primarily for leaders who are not in HR, let's briefly review the techniques available for sourcing candidates.

Job boards. All job boards are not created equal. Some will allow you to post jobs for free, because their goal is to be able to list the largest number of jobs. Other boards will charge, for example, $300 per month or $1 per click. When you're willing to pay, you'll get a lot more candidates. Boards also vary widely from super-broad ones that want every job listing everywhere, to super-niched ones for specialized roles.

Career site. The volume of applications coming to your career site is to some extent a function of the visibility of your brand. If you've worked hard on your brand, you can reap some of the rewards here. A few organizations really put an effort into creating elaborate career pages, explaining why an individual would want to work there and how great the culture is, and they work to make each job sound interesting. Other companies use it as a simple electronic bulletin board.

Referrals. As with career sites, the referral systems vary widely in organizations. Some are simple instructions about how employees can refer friends. Others are highly elaborate productions that talk about how one of the coolest things you can do at the company is to refer your friends.

We want to spend a moment really focusing on referrals, because there is so much potential for you to distinguish yourself and improve your hiring in short order.

It's a myth that you must have a paid rewards program in order to motivate people. In fact, as you'll see, it's also a cop-out.

Daniel: In the early 2000s I was running recruiting at my consulting company and we realized that when we got the occasional referral, it was great. I literally could hire an engineer for $120,000 and then put them on a project immediately where the customer was paying $250,000. *Let's do more of that.*

We created the standard type of referral program where we gave $1,000 to anyone who referred a person whom we eventually hired.

We weren't getting many referrals, so we increased the bonus. Then we increased it some more because we didn't have many takers.

We got to the point where we ran a monthly special: "$30,000 if we hire your friend."

It didn't move the needle.

Only years later, with the perspective that comes from being in the hiring business at Greenhouse, were a number of possible issues identified:

- We had in effect put a transactional price on someone's friendship, which may have been discomforting.
- We had very high standards for hiring, so that meant the vast majority of the few referrals we did get were not qualified. That could have made people uncomfortable whose referred friend got rejected: *Maybe I won't refer my other friends, only to have the same bad news delivered to them.*
- The new hire had to work for us for six months, so the reward was substantially separated from the action we wanted to encourage.
- We also felt that if a few people did end up getting the reward, they tended not to be very vocal about it, nor did we make any big deal about the reward.

We've since taken a very different approach at Greenhouse. We don't incentivize the outcome (someone getting hired); instead, we incentivize the activity of someone making a referral.

Every time someone at Greenhouse makes a referral, they immediately get a raffle ticket. It doesn't matter whether we hire the referred person or not. You're free to exchange the tickets for cool swag that can only be earned through a raffle ticket, and no other way. So, wearing the shirt makes a statement inside the company.

At the end of the year, we have a big all-hands meeting, where we put all the raffle tickets into a drum. The winner gets an all-expenses-paid vacation for two to go anywhere in the world.

Now people feel like wow, that's really extravagant. Yes, but we're only paying it once. So, instead of a $3,000-per-hire referral prize that generates no buzz, this costs a few thousand once a year for the entire program.

We also make sure to push referrals throughout the year: recognizing people each month who are earning raffle tickets, sending emails about the program, and so on.

We see to it that the employee making the referrals knows that we're treating the candidates well when they come in for an interview.

This simple shift from monetary reward to activity reward is a big unlock for people. It can get you 30–40 percent referral hires, instead of the 10–20 percent that's common at many companies.

Of course, you can't plug in a better referral program and expect it to do much, if your candidate experience sucks on every other dimension. All the elements we've been discussing in this book are interconnected. However, you have to start somewhere, and revamping your referral program is a project that will reward you handsomely, especially when you take steps to improve the interviewing process at the same time.

Agencies. Earlier we talked about the useful role agencies play. The good news is they typically take the financial risk because you pay nothing up front. The not-so-good news is that if you hire a candidate they delivered, you'll pay around 20 percent of the annual salary of that person. With agencies that focus on executive search, you'll pay them up front whether they find the right candidate or not.

Specialized sourcing software. Some organizations have used technology in creative ways to access discreet candidate pools. They can be excellent sources for candidates when diversity goals are not being met and you need more applicants at the top of the funnel. Even if you don't use Greenhouse, you're welcome to look at our large number of partners and contact them directly. Please visit https://www.greenhouse.io/integrations.

Cold outreach outbound sourcing. This is where you start from scratch and hit the phones, email, and any other communication method to contact strangers and ask if they're interested in working at your company. It's like what business development reps do in the sales and marketing world. The key is to personalize! Emphasize quality and building individual connections over "spray and pray" bulk emails.

Sourcing from database. If you've been doing the most basic relationship management, you'll have a database of people who have applied for jobs, and candidates whom you interviewed but who didn't get an offer. You'll also have lists of people you met at career events, meetups, reunions, and so on. Over time, this can become a tremendous asset. It may be worth staying in touch with these folks. Think about valuable or interesting content you have that you could share with them (ending them a newsy email once a quarter about the great things going on in your company, say) so they remember you when the time comes for them to look for their next job.

The Care and Feeding of Your Database

A database of potential candidates is different from the sorts of lists many businesses have. Let's say you run a retail furniture store and you collect names from events and past purchases. It's smart to stay in touch with those people with news and future promotions. That way when they're in the market for a sofa, you'll be "top of mind" by virtue of your steady communication.

It's different with a candidate database. People who applied or got interviews but no offers generally do not stick around waiting for your useful email or newsletter. They're on to other jobs after a while. Therefore the same type of long-term cultivation isn't quite as effective.

We see three good uses for these lists. First, when you have a candidate-sparse role, why not see who may happen to be available at the moment from your list? Second, campus recruiting is often a long game, where the candidate won't graduate for a year or more. It's definitely worth staying in touch with them, with emails tailored to that demographic.

(continued)

(*continued*)

Third, sometimes we'll have more than one really strong candidate for a job, though we only have one opening at the time. We call the other candidate a "silver medalist," at least internally. We make a special effort to stay in more personal touch with this small group of highly competitive candidates. Though it's true that they're likely to be snapped up in short order, you never know if they may be willing to join your organization if the mutual chemistry is great. Besides, they may have friends who are similarly qualified.

Internal. Companies that have a relatively young workforce need to focus here. Unlike earlier generations, people under 30 tend to think, *I can't see myself doing this same job for more than two years*. If you want to retain more of those people, you need to show them career paths within the organization and encourage them to apply when appropriate. As we'll discuss in Chapter 9, leaders need to set the tone that it's not only okay to move internally, but it's encouraged.

Social media. This is another case of tuning your sourcing efforts to match your target audience and job profile. Certain jobs are much more likely than others to have large numbers of potential candidates on social media all day long. However, depending on how candidate-sparse a job is, you may want to test this channel even if you think it may not bear fruit. Sometimes you may be surprised.

Don't think transactionally when posting to social media. If you post a job and tweet, "I'm hiring an engineer; click here," no one will click. The proper way to use social media for hiring is to build a community. Post interesting stuff, contribute to the community, and eventually your online business relationships can lead to qualified candidates.

Events. This label encompasses a lot of different efforts, many of which can be quite productive. We've already talked about campus recruiting.

Then there's what you might call community building, where you start or regularly attend a meetup. Live ones sometimes have several hundred members, and there are Slack communities of 10,000 members or more with a common interest. Invariably, in these events someone is looking for a new job.

Organizations will also get together and sponsor a career fair or open house, sometimes with interviews and offers made on the spot.

Although we group these different gatherings under events, we by no means want you to conclude that they're all the same. Hosting a meetup for senior engineers is much different from a fair for juniors in college. Therefore, when deciding on your sourcing plan, recognize the whole spectrum of variations even within one of these main categories.

When It Made Sense for Greenhouse to Hire an Agency

Not long ago, we wanted to hire a board member, and we don't hire board members very often. We wanted to hire a woman. We went to a specific group that places women on boards and we were willing to pay to have the right candidates. Building that capability ourselves wasn't worth an investment to do it, so in effect we rented the capability.

In contrast, we also hired six salespeople last year, and we're going to hire six more this next quarter and maybe every quarter after that. For us to spend $25,000 every time we hire a sales rep is wasteful and inefficient. Therefore, we've built that capability. We have an inside team that knows where to find good salespeople, what their detailed profile is like, and how to pitch to them. In addition, we have past salespeople who've been in our system but who, for one reason or another, didn't take the job. We can easily reach out to them. The takeaway: Don't decide to use only certain methods, and never use others as a matter of policy. Instead, decide what your strategic and tactical capabilities and needs are, and match the full range of options accordingly.

Putting These Concepts into Practice

In more than one place in this book, we've talked about the need to work on the business and not just work in it. Let's look a little more closely at the dynamics of that balance.

If you visit the Greenhouse site, you'll see that we have a plant motif throughout. That metaphor goes well beyond a nice design, and is highly relevant to our discussion at the moment.

Some techniques take a long time between when you plant the insignificant little seeds and when you see any results. It can almost seem like a waste of effort at the time. With some forethought and regular tending, they can bear abundant fruit, or turn into something mighty. Yet sometimes you're hungry for results and there is no luxury of time to think about planting.

Therefore, it's useful to take all the sourcing techniques we've mentioned, and put them on a continuum of time, as you see in Figure 6.2.

The row of Tactics in Figure 6.2 are the same ones we mentioned earlier in this chapter. For this discussion, look one row up, to the Strategy row.

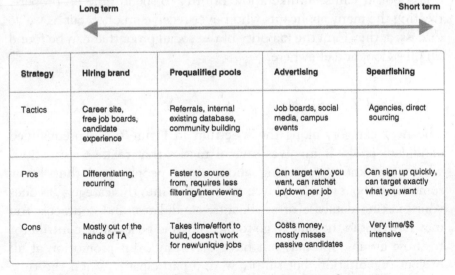

Strategy	Hiring brand	Prequalified pools	Advertising	Spearfishing
Tactics	Career site, free job boards, candidate experience	Referrals, internal existing database, community building	Job boards, social media, campus events	Agencies, direct sourcing
Pros	Differentiating, recurring	Faster to source from, requires less filtering/interviewing	Can target who you want, can ratchet up/down per job	Can sign up quickly, can target exactly what you want
Cons	Mostly out of the hands of TA	Takes time/effort to build, doesn't work for new/unique jobs	Costs money, mostly misses passive candidates	Very time/$$ intensive

Figure 6.2   How to Think About a Holistic Sourcing Strategy.

Hiring Brand

There are long-term strategies and short-term ones. One key long-term strategy is your hiring brand. If your brand is strong enough, people come to your career site because they want to work for your company. The good news is that this feels like effortless sourcing when your brand is that good. It can be recurring, even for decades in some cases. The problem is that this use of brand awareness is mostly out of the hands of your talent acquisition (TA) team—recruiters cannot do much to influence the brand in the mass market.

Sometimes, a company can get famous in a hurry, if it gets out-sized media attention. As attractive as that sounds, it can be highly dangerous for the company: Hiring seems effortless and it can all come crashing down, as we'll discuss in Chapter 8.

If the brand is strong enough, then candidates will come in even via the free, massive job boards. You're well enough known that you basically get candidates every which way.

Another long-term strategy is to build your candidate-experience brand, for when someone who doesn't know you looks you up on Glassdoor. It can seem like a low priority to spend time on properly treating the many applicants who never receive an offer, but as we've discussed, they form the majority of the social proof that can be found on Glassdoor and elsewhere.

Prequalified Talent Pools

The next category along the spectrum in Figure 6.2 is prequalified candidate pools. It involves several tactics that relate to situations where you know something about these people, and they know something about you. Employee referrals fall into this category, as does your existing database of applicants, candidates, and contacts. You may have put in the time to go to meetups and be a visible contributor to those groups. You may not have done any overt promotion at all of your organization, but simply were a participant. When the time comes, you and anyone else in the group like you can tap that network with the occasional mention of an opening.

Please note that these strategies do not have distinct boundaries but can overlap. Building prequalified groups can take almost as long as building a brand but in general may result in a faster payoff, because you're focused on smaller groups and not on the world at large. And the payoff can indeed be great: you put the word out, and a large number of people who can vouch for you to some extent may apply or tell their friends.

If you're trying to fill roles that these groups have no experience in, then their vouching for you will be more limited, along the lines of "I don't know about that position, but from what I've seen, the company is solid." Still not a bad endorsement.

One issue is this category can be problematic from a diversity perspective: If you're sourcing from your existing employee base, and if the existing base isn't that diverse, then the talent you get may not help matters.

That may not be an issue if the prequalified pools are just one of your sourcing techniques. Also, you can use timing to your advantage. Let's say you're looking to hire female engineers, and you know your internal database has a lower percentage of them than you'd like. In that case, you can post the position first in other channels that tend to have higher proportions of women, and only post it to your internal database later if necessary.

DE&I is a Win/Win at Checkr

Checkr is a forward-thinking company. It helps companies to modernize their background-check process with technology and products that make hiring safer, more efficient, and more inclusive. But Checkr is also doing groundbreaking work inside its own company. We spoke with Daniel Yanisse, co-founder and CEO, and Arthur Yamamoto, VP of Talent, about two things they do to create diversified pools of talent.

(continued)

(*continued*)

1. We Became a Fair Chance Employer

The background check process is quite strict and conservative. Many background check decisions are binary, based on whether a person has criminal records. If you look at statistics in the United States, about a third of Americans have some sort of criminal record in their background, whether it's a minor record, or a DUI, or more severe types. You can imagine that if a third of people have a criminal record and every time there's a flag, they likely get rejected from an opportunity, that leaves a lot of people without good job opportunities.

That is a continuing problem. We try to break this negative cycle, where people make a mistake and pay for it—whether they serve time or pay fines—and then they're penalized a second time, when they try to get a job. We worked to develop software that lets customers have a more nuanced decision process. Our data show that having more open background check criteria allows companies to get great talent, to get access to more talent, and to get really good retention quality of employees and workers.

We also decided to become a Fair Chance Employer. It means giving second chances to people with criminal records. We've been able to hire some amazing talent. When you have a discussion with a person who made a mistake in the past and discuss their background, you can do your own assessment as well to understand whether there is still a risk, or whether the person has learned from this experience and is rehabilitated.

We've found that the people we hired this way are really dedicated to the company, very grateful for the opportunity, and sincerely want to prove themselves to succeed in life and be able to make the most of this special opportunity. Overall,

(*continued*)

(*continued*)

we've seen higher performance, higher retention, very positive engagement, and a benefit to our culture when we started to give second chances to people to join our company.

2. We Make Our Interview Process as Fair as Possible

We're all about hiring the best talent, but at the same time we're all about giving that talent equitable exposure in the hiring process. Therefore, before you can make any offer at Checkr as a hiring manager, you must bring in at least two candidates who meet our criteria for diversity. For us, that means that the candidate either doesn't identify as male or is in an underrepresented group. For us in San Francisco, that means African American, Latin American, or Native American. In cities like Denver, where Asian Americans are underrepresented, we count them in as well.

Our approach was tied to research that we saw around university professors. The research found that for women who applied to be professors, if they were one candidate out of four, they had almost no chance of being hired. If it was two out of four, it was still less than a 50 percent chance, and when you stack the deck and had three out of four, then the odds started to even out a bit. For us, it just became about making the process as fair as possible. We stacked the deck with candidates so that hiring managers saw a really diverse slate of candidates before they made a decision, and then we would let them make the right decision for their team and their business from there.

It's yielded some great results for us. Within one of our IT teams, early on the team was small, and we were looking to build it out. The manager had a great referral who was someone they had worked with, who was ready to work, and ready to accept an

(*continued*)

(*continued*)

offer immediately. It happened to be a white male, and the team needed the help immediately. We said, "There are no exceptions." We pushed them into the process, at the risk of losing that referral candidate. The recruiting team took on the pressure of moving things as quickly and smoothly as possible while maintaining a great candidate experience.

We brought in two more candidates. One was a Latin male, and the other was an Asian female, and both did great in the process. The hiring manager ultimately loved all three candidates, pushed to get additional headcount, and we brought all three on. So he got his referral, still built out a diverse team, and we got all the IT resources we needed as a company. It was a win-win for everyone.

Advertising

With this strategy you fish in specific pools, on a pay-to-fish basis. This is a popular approach because you have a lot of control: You can dial up or down the exposure, as well as focus on distinct groups like diversity job boards.

Obviously, the downside is that it costs money. Also, you mostly get people who are out looking for jobs. That's not necessarily a bad thing, given how often people switch jobs. However, there are plenty of great people who are not looking for a job but who would consider yours, if they knew about it. If you only advertise, you miss this large segment.

Spearfishing

As the name implies, this is where you go after individual people. You can do this yourself, or hire an agency. The benefit is that you can target exactly the kind of person you want. It can work to fill both existing and new roles, and can of course help you to meet any diversity goals.

You can get spearfishing going quickly as well. The downside is that it will cost you a lot of time, or money, or both, depending on how extensively you use it.

Now's the Next-Best Time

If you are forever working in and not on the business, the scope of your options will forever remain narrow. You may want to diversify your organization with many more women in technical positions, for example. The best thing to do: 20 years ago you would have started and cultivated a site for women engineers, and by now it could be the premier site of its kind. Then you could be reaping benefits year after year, based on the mini brand and the following you built.

The next best thing is to start now, with an intentional plan that extends beyond immediate payments for immediate payoffs. It doesn't preclude you from also doing some short-term things to meet your goals.

Three Necessary Actions

As a leader in the organization, you need to make sure that three things (among others) get done if you want to be great at hiring:

1. **You need to invest appropriately across the continuum.** The filter-feeder want-ad approach will doom you to mediocrity. The key words here are "across the continuum," so make sure you don't just have one or two pet methods. Have the discussion with the head of recruiting about which long-term and medium-term initiatives are being actively worked. There should be latitude about which techniques are chosen, but in our opinion, it is risky and costly to live only in the short-term end of the continuum.
2. **Modulate your approaches, based on the job.** It's fine to be doing some things at no cost, like certain job boards, your career site, and so on. But have a proactive conversation about which jobs should get the budget, and which techniques you maybe have underutilized in the past.

3. **Rise and grind.** Unlike the recruiter we mentioned in Chapter 1, whose sourcing plan involved clicking a button in the ATS, to be great at hiring means that you'll be doing some hard work. Your competitors get a vote in your marketplace for talent. If they're willing to invest, cultivate candidates, and try multiple techniques, then that level of effort becomes the price of admission to get your share of the top talent. It's hard work, but also smart work in the sense of the more you grind and experiment, the better you perform.

How You Measure Success

If you're taking the actions we mentioned above, there are four factors that combine to give you a handle on whether your efforts are paying off. If you as a leader can monitor these measurements, they'll give you a good sense of the situation.

1. **Quality versus quantity.** It's not that helpful if you get 500 candidates for a job, nor if you only get three candidates. You should seek the sweet spot. What is that location, exactly? It depends on the job. For candidate-dense roles, which tend to require less experience and are more easily replaced, the number can be smaller. If you're opening a new role or it's a very specialized one, you may need many more candidates in order to find the right fit.
2. **Speed.** How quickly are you finding qualified candidates? Is it within days of opening the job, or does it drag on for months? Depending on the role and how far you plan ahead for filling it, you may be fine with two months to fill it, or two months could put you out of business. Have the discussion, preferably before the role opens up, and now you'll have a useful benchmark.
3. **Resources.** Where do you spend your time and money? Less is not always better, if you're investing in some efforts that may take some time to pay off, or if your competitors are willing to write the big checks to source the best talent.
4. **Diversity.** What is the makeup of your candidate group? How does that compare to what you want it to be, both in the short term and longer term? If you haven't met your goals, are you measuring to see if you're on a trajectory to meet them within a reasonable time? If not, you should reevaluate your mix of sourcing techniques.

How to Boost Your Diversity Referral Program

The natural thing that happens is that most employee referral programs reinforce the makeup of your existing organization. That's because most social and professional networks we belong to reflect our own identity. If your company is mostly male and white, it's not surprising that when you ask them for referrals, they will give you mostly male, white referrals. The same would be true of any ethnic group.

One company tackled this phenomenon in a very interesting way. By simply diversifying the kinds of requests that they made of their employees for referrals, they got a more diverse and stronger employee referral flow.

Instead of saying, "Hey, if you refer someone to us and we hire them, you'll get points," they tried something different. One month they would say to all of their engineers, "Who's the best woman you've ever worked with?" Next month they would say to their employees, 'We're looking for more customer support managers who are people of color. Whom do you know who's good?" Asking people for more specifics helps to overcome bias and generate more candidate volume.

There's also a huge difference in results, based on the specific way you ask questions. If you say, "We're looking for great women engineers. Do you know anyone?" that's a yes/no question, and it's easy for someone to spend five seconds to say "No." Instead, you will get much more useful information if you ask, "Who's the best woman engineer you know?" There's no "no" answer to that, so it makes people think more about the answer.

Also, when they try to answer that question, most people go through their mental Rolodex, and they can hold about seven people in their head. Instead, it's better if you sit with them and look at their LinkedIn network, with the hundreds of people they are connected to. In that case, they'll be like, "Oh, I forgot about that person!" That's because you can't possibly recall hundreds of people spontaneously.

Internal Referrals and Diversity

Many organizations have internal job boards that list all the available jobs. Employees can apply to those jobs and are usually treated separately from an external applicant. They're given preferential treatment because they're a known quantity.

What companies figured out is that only a small percentage of employees ever become active in the program and apply for a job. Or these people may read about a job, contact a buddy, and say, "Hey, I think you might be great for this job. Why don't you apply?" Sometimes people will get jobs this way without going through the interview process. Sidestepping that critical process can result in less-qualified people getting the job.

Instead, some forward-thinking companies are creating what could be called an internal talent marketplace. They build a database of all employees by asking about and documenting their skills. They also note if employees say they're willing to relocate, or what departments they would consider working in.

That way they can scan across the entire employee base and identify people who might be a potential match. Then they can contact them and make them aware of the positions available. It not only eliminates reliance on somebody happening to think of a friend as a possible candidate, but it also avoids the problem of internal applicants being viewed as disloyal to their current managers. After all, the company asked the employee if they might be interested in the other job.

This kind of program taps a talent pool that's effectively unknown to recruiters. They may anecdotally know about the past histories and talents of some employees, but not across the board and especially not when the organization reaches 1,000 employees or more. We see this internal mining happening at the most-advanced companies, but there's no reason why it could not be replicated at any size organization.

The Ultimate Measure of Success

We talked earlier about how you can measure your success by looking at the four dimensions of quality/quantity, speed, resources used, and diversity. When your multi-channel sourcing engine is up and running with those four measurements looking good, you'll enjoy a special byproduct of it all: confidence.

It's an amazing feeling to have the serene confidence that you can hire great people whenever you need them, quickly and reliably. You're fully aware that great people won't be content with swimming for their entire careers in a pond, so you know they'll be moving on. That's not a scary thought but an intriguing one: now you get to attract the next talented person who will help to make your goals a reality.

Notes

1. https://www.monticello.org/site/research-and-collections/i-am-great-believer-luckspurious-quotation.
2. https://en.wikipedia.org/wiki/PayPal_Mafia.

Chapter 6: Takeaways

The world has changed from the want-ad days. Don't be a filter feeder, waiting for some applicants to come by. You need a comprehensive plan to attract talent.

Also, don't send one-size-fits-all emails to targeted talent. You need to stand out from the crowd. Great hiring is like great marketing: You need an organized, systematic, and measurable system.

Forget the one-and-done sourcing of the past. It now must be a continuous process, given the high mobility of your best talent. You must be able to attract great talent at will. To do that:

- Take a portfolio approach versus one favorite sourcing method. That means investing appropriately across the continuum.
- Optimize and improve each sourcing channel.
- Try harder in order to stand above the competition.
- Match the sourcing technique to the role being filled.

Measure success using several factors:

- First, look at the **quality versus quantity** of each of your sourcing channels. This may help to optimize your efforts toward those channels that actually deliver the candidates you end up hiring.

- Next, measure **how quickly you find candidates.** It allows you to monitor this key indicator over time so you can improve it. Also, this data will allow you to improve the accuracy of future estimates to meet hiring goals.
- Keep track of **resources needed to fill roles,** and break the numbers out by type of role instead of having one average number. Monitoring this will not only improve forecasts, but can be an indicator of sourcing channels that should be deemphasized in favor of more productive ones.
- Regularly measure **hiring against your diversity goals.** This is an area that tends to take time, so regular monitoring will let you know if you're on track, or whether a course correction is in order.

When you can execute on this system, it gives you the confidence that you can attract the best talent at will, and that changes everything.

Expert Insights: Joelle Emerson

Please tell us about your background.

I've always been passionate about equity and justice. I started my career as a civil rights and women's rights lawyer, suing companies for things like pay and promotion discrimination, pregnancy discrimination, sexual harassment, and retaliation. In the course of doing that work, I began to feel like this reactive approach—suing a company after so many things had gone wrong—wasn't inspiring the level of impact I wanted to see in organizations.

I fundamentally believe that organizations can be powerful tools for creating a better, more inclusive world, and I wanted to find a way to drive that change. Ultimately, I founded Paradigm alongside Natalie Johnson, who developed and analyzed a wide range of diversity and inclusion initiatives at Google, and Dr. Carissa Romero, who co-founded Stanford University's applied research center on learning mindsets. We partner with organizations around the world that want to build best-in-class cultures where people from all backgrounds can do their best work and can thrive.

Hiring is one critical aspect of diversity, equity, and inclusion (DE&I) efforts: It directly influences representation within organizations, and it is a core process where organizations have an opportunity to embed equity and inclusion into their decision-making. Over the past several years, we've partnered with hundreds of companies on a wide range of hiring initiatives, from building more inclusive,

140

structured hiring processes to training people that make hiring decisions.

You've been an advocate of a structured approach to hiring for a long time, is that right?

We have always been huge advocates of structured interview processes: defining criteria in advance, aligning interview questions with those criteria, and having people write down how they're evaluating candidates. Although Paradigm and Greenhouse had been on each other's radars for quite some time, when Jon and I bumped into each other at a mutual client's office and got to talking, we recognized that our philosophies were very aligned around what inclusive hiring looks like. The nice thing about inclusive hiring is that it's also better hiring—that's one thing Jon and I both felt strongly about.

There's this assumption that the more information an interviewer has about a candidate the better. But that's not your approach, is it?

We take a different approach. We recommend that organizations first determine what information each decision maker in the process needs; then that decision maker should only have the information that they need to make a good decision.

For example, some organizations share a candidate's referral status with the people conducting the interviews. That has a huge potential to create bias with interviewers. If I know that this person was referred by Jon, and I think Jon's amazing, I'm probably going to give this candidate the benefit of the doubt. On the other hand, I'm going to interview differently another person whom I don't know, and who isn't in my extended network.

We recommend giving only the details the interviewer needs, which may not even be the full résumé—just the key data points related to what they should be evaluating.

Could you describe the preparation you take before conducting interviews?

For every role you're hiring for, determine the key competencies that you need to assess. Then for each of those competencies, decide which interviewer is best suited to assess them.

From there, determine the questions you need to ask in order to assess for each competency. For each question, create a rubric to evaluate candidates' answers. In other words, determine in advance what a great answer to the question looks like, and also what a good answer looks like, and what a poor answer looks like.

Most organizations miss this step, but a wealth of research shows that if we start an interview without a clear set of interview questions and responses, we will interpret candidates' answers very differently depending on our preexisting biases, assumptions, and shortcuts.

Let's say I ask you to walk me through how you would approach gathering feedback from multiple stakeholders for a product update. If I know that a great answer should include a multipart process for gathering the feedback, then I'll be listening for that in a candidate's answer. If I haven't thought about what makes a great answer, I might hear their responses through the lens of all of my preexisting biases and assumptions, or I may get swept up in whether they communicate the way that I do, or if they are charismatic, all of which may not really be relevant to this particular role.

One recommendation we've made in this book is whenever you're evaluating someone on a scorecard element, it's a best practice to add a little comment to the rating at the time. That way, when you're in the roundup, you remember why you rated the person that way. Would you say that's something that should always be done, or should it be optional?

I definitely think that should always be done because one of the best checks on bias is asking people to explain the reasons for their decisions. This applies to hiring, promotions, assigning a high visibility opportunity to someone, or a host of other decisions. It's a quick check to make sure we have reasons for our decisions. It makes us really reflect on our reasoning, both in the moment and then when we come back to discuss it.

For example, let's say I was a strong "no" on "problem solving skills," but in the debrief, my manager speaks first and they're a strong "yes." I'm more likely to think: Well, I wasn't really sure; I guess they were fine. If it's written down, then whoever's facilitating that debrief can say, "Joelle, you were a strong 'no' immediately after your interview, and here's what you wrote."

I could imagine that someone might raise an objection and say that all we're doing is asking people to double down on their opinions and justify them firmly. I think we are. We want to push people to really think, "Did I have a reason to support this?" It can be so easy to just go through and check yes or no or I don't know.

If people are given an opportunity to rate candidates as neutral, a lot of people will use that. We really want to push people to make a decision and to justify that decision, so that we don't get into a debrief room and have groups lean toward whatever the first person says, or whatever the senior hiring manager says. The whole reason for having multiple interviewers is to have multiple perspectives. Having those perspectives grounded in something more than just an initial gut instinct is pretty important.

How do we create a hiring culture that is fairer and more inclusive? What's your message to leaders?

I really encourage leaders to reflect on what they are trying to accomplish with their hiring, what diversity really means, and why it's important.

Most organizations absolutely need to increase representation of different identities in their company, but "diversity" should not be a check-the-box part of your hiring strategy. There is no such thing as an inherently "diverse candidate." Diversity is a state that applies to groups of things and groups of people. If you have six orange gummy bears, and I give you a red gummy bear, a red gummy bear isn't intrinsically diverse. It's that the orange group was homogenous, and this red gummy bear adds something different to the group. We want a diverse group: We need orange gummy bears, but we also need red ones and green ones.

Most leaders agree with this in principle, but fail to realize how their biases misalign with their intentions. A lot of the work that we do with leaders is highlighting the research that consistently shows that—unless we have a structured process, and unless we're really intentional about inclusion—we tend to make concessions for the folks that are from the majority. We tend to apply less scrutiny to people that look like the folks we already have on our team—those orange gummy bears—and tend to apply a higher level of scrutiny to people that come from underrepresented backgrounds. For success, you need to cast a wide net and create a fair process that produces equitable outcomes that should also—if we've done it well—be diverse.

Then you need to consider whether you are a place where people from underrepresented backgrounds will want to work. How are you talking about people and talent? What do your job descriptions look like? What does your website look like? These send powerful messages to prospective applicants about what your workplace is like. It's worthwhile to think about whom you want to attract, and be as intentional as you can about the signals you're sending.

If you look at companies on the spectrum: ones that are doing nothing—we know what they look like. But, if you look at the best examples that you can think of, what do they look like? What are their challenges moving ahead with DE&I, versus your average company?

A strong signal that an organization is on the right track is when they're using data to identify and focus on the barriers within their own organization, rather than getting swept up in comparing themselves to other organizations. There is no one-size-fits-all approach to DEI, and what drives one organization may not address the issues that another is facing. There is certainly value in looking at external benchmarks, but the most advanced companies are focused on how their current state compares to where they were a year ago—not how they compare to their peers.

The advanced companies tend to have pretty good buy-in because they've made their values clear. However, companies are made up of individuals. I've worked with clients who were excellent in many respects, and then you had one manager who did something harmful or was not aligned with the company's values. Sometimes, it's two steps forward and one step back.

Expert Insights: Porter Braswell

Please share a bit of your background, and specifically the founding story of your company.

I am the CEO and co-founder of Jopwell, the leading career advancement platform for Black, Latinx, and Native American students and professionals. Jopwell was born when my co-founder, Ryan Williams, and I were working in finance. In addition to our day-to-day jobs on the trading floor, we were often asked to support diversity recruiting efforts at our company. Ryan and I saw a disconnect; in finance, and across other industries, recruiting and hiring teams said they didn't know how to reach communities of color, which created a concerning absence of a clear hiring pipeline. We knew there had to be a way to attract diverse talent at scale. So, we left Wall Street to build Jopwell. Jopwell has facilitated tens of thousands of connections between our community and over 300 partner organizations, including Spotify, UBS, and the PGA.

What comes to mind regarding things that organizations often get wrong about their diversity initiatives, and that ultimately lead to a lack of diversity?

Organizations often make diversity, equity, and inclusion (DE&I) initiatives the responsibility of one person or one team, and it shouldn't be. For diversity initiatives to be successful, leaders within the organization need to play an active role and set the tone for company-wide participation and support. Organizations recognize they have challenges pertaining to DE&I, but they often don't invest the time to understand those challenges or their roots. By skipping the diagnostic phase, organizations will struggle to make long-lasting change and will instead have temporary success only to be back at square one down the line. Building a diverse company requires intentionality and support from the entire organization. It's important for an organization to commit to DE&I as a priority, and to setting goals, finding the right resources (both internal and external partners), and being transparent about the progress being made.

Do you have suggestions for useful actions a leader can take to improve DE&I in their company?

Here are a few steps leaders can take:

Define diversity and why it matters. Always start with the "why" to help bring people along. It shouldn't be assumed that everyone appreciates the importance of diverse perspectives and backgrounds, so it's up to leaders to articulate why it matters to the organization. Once leaders have articulated the why, communicate it to the full team so everyone is aware of the organization's stance and commitment.

In tandem with this, clearly articulate what diversity means to the organization. Being able to clearly define the pain points the organization experiences and the groups of individuals that require better representation is a critical first step in an organization's diversity, equity, and inclusion journey.

Once the why and the what are clear, an organization can work to collect metrics and feedback to provide a starting point for their DE&I journey. After the baseline is developed, then leaders should map out milestones, goals, and timelines for diversity efforts based on the desires of leadership and the overall team. During this phase, it's important to set timelines and to be transparent to hold the organization and leadership accountable.

There is still a pervasive perception that diversity is a pipeline problem. What are your thoughts about scaling talent pipelines for under-represented groups?

Ryan and I set out to create Jopwell to specifically tackle the "pipeline" problem. Jopwell is in its fifth year and we have facilitated tens of thousands of connections between our members and our partners—proving that the talent DOES exist—and in very large numbers across all sectors and experience levels. Organizations need to invest time and resources to prove their commitment to DE&I and to create a culture that supports their initiatives. This will allow organizations to authentically connect and engage with diverse talent, which will make them an employer of choice for communities of color, subsequently scaling talent pipelines.

Expert Insights: Katie Burke

HubSpot is a leader in being transparent and active with its DE&I initiatives. We spoke with Katie Burke, Chief People Officer at HubSpot, which has more than 3,000 employees.

HubSpot's journey toward becoming a more diverse company is well-known. What are some of the things you did to accelerate diversity in sourcing?

I don't think people talk enough about the fact that really some of the most important work you can do in building more diverse teams is to focus on the skills and attributes you really need for a role versus relying upon, for example, degrees, years of experience, how well someone knows something, or how flashy someone is. We try to train interviewers to seek out and assess those skills in objective ways.

At HubSpot, we do our best wherever possible to eliminate credentials or time limits that don't actually matter, like "Five years of experience. Bachelor's degree or equivalent required." I will admit that I was someone who grew up saying: "Years of experience is a good proxy. We want someone who's done this work before." A good recruiter pushed me to think when they said, "The five years of experience is really just a proxy for this skill that you need."

If you are a proficient project manager, it actually shouldn't matter to me whether you have five years of experience or 50 years of experience. The excellence of project management is really the skill I'm looking for. If you hire a lot of people, it's in your best interest to realize that you can still get the things that you really value in a candidate without using the traditional crutches we use to get them.

There's a ton of great research on the corporate skills gap and how it's developed over time. One of the biggest problems that occurred over time is degree inflation. A Harvard study found that 67 percent of job postings required a bachelor's degree or higher, yet just 16 percent of workers already in that position held such a degree. We use education as a proxy for experience or skill, and doing that has huge negative implications, not just for race but also socioeconomic diversity—access to more rural areas in the United States.

It's an important distinction to really push ourselves to go, "What is the skill someone actually needs," versus assuming that a degree is what gives you that skill. Honestly, it's a hard conversation to have with hiring managers. This is often a tough sell at organizations where folks are really proud of their education. But what you have to remind yourself is eliminating years of experience or a BA requirement does absolutely nothing to devalue your personal experience.

7

Making Confident, Informed Hiring Decisions

If we had to pick one aspect of hiring that's the most emblematic of all the things we advocate, it's interviewing.

In our experience in dealing with many thousands of organizations, we can say this with slight overstatement but a high level of confidence:

Everybody hates standard interviewing.

To be slightly more nuanced about it, we've all had situations where we thought we hit the ball out of the park in an interview. So, we acknowledge the occasional exception to the rule. But as a rule, the interview experience and usefulness at most organizations is pathetic.

We're going to fix that. In fact, we're not just going to eliminate the problems so that interviewing becomes some non-bad activity; we will show you how it can become the cornerstone of your ability to hire great talent at will.

Please don't be tempted to skip this chapter or to skim it because you think it's too much "in the weeds" and you don't need to know it. Leaders and hiring managers who attract great talent know that the better their interviewing process, the better the information they have on which to base hiring decisions.

How Bad Is Typical Interviewing? Let Us Count the Ways

First, it's useful to take a brief look at what makes typical interviewing so painful for so many people.

The fundamental problem is that there is no plan for what to do before, during, or after the interview.

Somebody contacts the applicant and gives too little information about how to prepare for the interview, as we discussed in Chapter 5. The candidate is stressed out for no good reason, even before the interview happens.

Somebody grabs an employee who may or may not be good for conducting this particular interview, because there was no plan around that. The interviewer is told, "Here a résumé. You're going to meet with this person in 15 minutes. Tell me if they're good."

The interviewer is given zero training or instructions about what they're supposed to ask. So, they just make stuff up. Or they use the same favorite questions, regardless of the role or candidate. Because there is no plan for questioning, the chances are quite good that questions can range from irrelevant to downright illegal. And because there is no coordination between interviewers, the hours of interviews result in lots of duplicate questions, and important areas for discussion are entirely missed.

Because the hiring manager often feels like they can delegate hiring to the recruiters, they don't make interviewing a priority. That leaves the recruiter to wonder if the hiring manager will show up to the interview late, or not at all.

The hiring manager has not spent much time to get the recruiter up to speed on the details about the job, including how it differs from other similar jobs. The recruiter also doesn't know the common jargon, so the conversation with the candidate is superficial. When the candidate asks what the next steps are, the answer is vague because the next steps are vague.

An interviewer walks out and the recruiter says, "So, what did you think?" The answer might be "She seems smart; I like her."

Ugh. And we haven't even discussed the whole decision-making process, which is equally dysfunctional. We'll get to that later in this chapter.

No one set out to engineer a lousy interview experience. Nobody walked into the interview room with the intention of asking irrelevant or illegal questions. For the most part, everyone in the dysfunctional experience wants to be a professional. It's just that chaos fills the vacuum left when there's no system.

The Boss as Expert

The common thing that happens especially in early-stage start-ups—or in places where you don't trust the process—is that the hiring manager does all the early-stage interviews. They don't trust anybody else to make a decision. They feel this way because when their organization was small they did all the hiring, so it's their baby.

It turns out that most people have overconfidence in their ability to predict all kinds of things. But even if you are objectively good at hiring, it's not scalable. Your ability to make good decisions about hiring isn't all that relevant, any more than Bill Gates being good at programming was the secret to Microsoft's enduring growth. That's not how it works.

You need to work through other people in order to scale. If you properly train other people to play their role, you'll still be involved. But you'll be doing three interviews at the end, in order to make the final decision, instead of 30 interviews at the top of the funnel.

The Science of Decision-Making

Your ability to hire great talent goes beyond fixing the issues we identified above. It also depends on the quality of the decisions you make.

And you *do* make a great deal of decisions when you hire someone. Unfortunately, most decisions that hiring teams make are done with very little evidence, and not in a rational, repeatable way.

We're not just talking the decision to hire someone; the same issue applies to decisions that are made higher up in the funnel:

- Where should we spend our hiring budget?
- Which roles should we open first?
- Where should we advertise these roles?
- How much money is it worth it to us to find ten more candidates?

- Should we broaden our sourcing channels?
- Which of these candidates should we move forward with?
- What questions should we ask the candidates?

People grapple with these and other questions as they fill a role. Very few of the questions get the benefit of rigorous thinking; instead, stuff just sort of gets decided the way it always has.

The reality is that in the absence of clear criteria and structures for decision-making, bias tends to creep in. All sorts of pernicious stuff gets in the way. For example, while we are walking to the interview room, if I crack a joke and you laugh, my first impression may be really positive. I just might spend the next 59 minutes confirming that first impression. At least, I'll probably rank you higher than I will the candidate who didn't get my joke.

Decisions Are Fragile Things

If you think about how long humans have been around, an extremely small amount of that time has been spent in modern industrial society or even organized agriculture. A few thousand generations were spent wondering just how close the saber-toothed tiger got to our cave last night.

In other words, up until very recently, the human brain has needed to make instant decisions that involved life and death. Using all your senses to evaluate danger has been a pretty useful survival mechanism. I have five milliseconds to decide if that thing that moved over there is a bear or just rustling leaves. It's life-saving to make those sorts of snap judgments, because in those situations *there is no other information* to consider.

But now we live in a world with lots of information and the ability to design systems. The advanced portion of our brains knows that we're hiring an engineer and we have four days—not four seconds—to decide. But the ancient survival mechanisms of our brains still give us instantaneous judgments about that tiger/engineer.

Biases Are Natural; Be Aware of Them

There's not much we can do about rewiring our brain evolution that has served our species well over the ages. But what we can do to adapt those ancient mechanisms to modern society is to be aware when certain processes happen, so we can choose to listen to that intuition—also known as bias—or ignore it.

For example, there's a "like me" bias, where I generally like people who are similar to me: They look similar, went to the same schools I did, grew up the same way I did, and talk the way I do. That may be an ancient mechanism and that's okay—except when it becomes a basis for hiring people instead of facts forming that basis.

Other common biases are the "halo effect" and "horn effect" where we grab onto a positive or negative aspect of the candidate and let it influence the rest of our judgment about that person. There is no shortage of biases that can sometimes creep into our thinking. A good article about some of them can be found at https://harver.com/blog/hiring-biases/.

Follow the Leader

Some brain processes work when we're alone and others kick in when we're in groups. We might rationally assume that if you add more people to a group, they will make better decisions. It turns out that certain problems creep in when groups try to make decisions.

We've all been in situations where a bunch of people are in a room, and if the person with the most perceived power or seniority states their opinion first, it generally tends to result in people agreeing with that opinion. That goes for hiring decisions and product launch decisions, as well as for minor things like what is a good name for something or the color we should paint the boardroom.

When it's a minor decision, then this is no big deal. But when it comes to hiring decisions, it is a big deal, and it can defeat the whole purpose of having multiple people interview a candidate.

Shifting Criteria

Another problematic situation involves shifting criteria. Let's say you want to hire a police chief.[1] You get a bunch of résumés and interview two finalists: a male and a female. The male has all the right certifications and education but not a lot of experience, and the female has a ton of experience but not the right educational experience.

So, whom should we hire? Some people may say, "Oh, the man." Why do you say that? "It's because I think education is the more important factor."

But if you run this as a careful experiment, and you just reverse the résumés, you'll get subjects who say you should hire the male because experience is the most important factor.

It turns out that people will sometimes shift the criteria that they say are most important, not based on just the facts but instead to fit a preconceived conclusion.

What's really interesting is if at the beginning you can get people to commit up front which is most important—education or experience—and only then you show them the résumés, they'll pick the one that's consistent with their commitment, regardless of applicant gender. It's a way to combat that shifting criteria thing.

As a leader, you should look for mechanisms that combat bias among you and your teams. Is it because you're trying to be a do-gooder and your teams are messed up? No. It's because bias is literally the definition of non-random systematic error. Optical illusions are an example of your brain systematically coming to the wrong conclusion about the real world. If you can eliminate or minimize those errors, you'll make better, more rational decisions about hiring and everything else.

So, what is a good decision? An irrelevant decision is to find and hire people that look like me. A good decision is to hire people who are the best at the job.

How do I apply more of my effort toward hiring people who are good at the job? A big step in that direction is to lay out your criteria ahead of time, instead of afterward, or implicitly. Commit to those criteria as a group. Then assign specific roles within the group as to who's going to do what in the decision-making process. You then solicit feedback independently and only consider the feedback collectively as a group after everyone's had a chance to do independent evaluations.

As you open roles and you interview for them, be continually alert for signs that mechanisms other than fact-based judgments are at work. Look hard at your processes if they are delivering unusual results. For example, why is it that at this one interview stage we seem to be weeding out a disproportionate number of women? The goal is not to "fix" the number to fit some preconceived notion about how many women are getting through. The goal is to be hiring the best people despite our human cauldrons of intuition and other processes. It's a never-ending effort to identify and remove non-random systematic error from our judgments and improve our decisions.

Your Systematic Process

How do we use all this awareness of how we can go astray to help us to design a process for great hiring? A great place to start is by adopting a progression of steps that you ensure people follow whenever a role opens.

Your first action should not be to post a job, no matter how much that feels like forward progress. Instead, the first action needs to be creating a plan. That task starts with the hiring manager, who should fill out the information below.

Recruiting Kickoff Collaboration

Details Summary

Title:

Hiring Manager:

Team:

Level:

Location:

Years of Experience:

Comp:

Ideal Start Date:

Pre-Kickoff Meeting Homework

What is the business need for opening this role? If you've hired for this position before, how has the role/team/scope of responsibilities changed since then? How will what this role will accomplish be different from what other teammates are working on?

What are the high-level objectives for this person? What goals need to be achieved a year from now for you to determine the hire is successful?

How will this role enable the team to meet its goals? In what ways will this hire affect the org in the next year?

What are the first 90-day goals for this person? For a superstar to accomplish what you said above in a year, what do they need to do in the first 90 days? Think about what this person will own, learn, and need to master.

How will success be measured? In other words, how will we know the above goals have been achieved?

Define the person who can achieve these goals.
  1. What non-negotiable skills/experiences do they need to have?
  2. What's coachable or nice-to-have?
  3. What personality traits enable someone to be successful in this role?

Would other companies/teams outside of ours describe this role differently? If so, how? Are there other titles that would describe the same thing? Would our title mean other things to other companies?

What are the team responsibilities? Who will this person report to?
Will this person manage anyone right away, or within the year?
Who will this person work most closely with? Who will they work
with cross-departmentally? Please name key individuals.
Who internally/externally depends on this person's output?

What is the sourcing plan? Provide a sample ideal profile, preferably
a link to a LinkedIn profile.
What is the target list of companies to prospect from?
Is industry experience very important for this position (i.e., Tech,
SaaS, HR, etc.)?
Is start-up/hyper-growth experience necessary for this position?
What are résumé non-starters?
What are the preferred education and certifications, if any?

What is the diversity sourcing plan? The recruiting team will priori-
tize diversity sourcing efforts while prospecting candidates. During the
kickoff meeting, let's discuss what "diversity" looks like for your team.
What are recommended diversity sourcing, job board, and event
resources?

How to sell this role? Why would anyone leave their current company to come work for us in this role? What is the career ladder or
anticipated progression for this position?

The Importance of this Homework

It's useful to anticipate that in an organization existing at the chaotic
or inconsistent level, a hiring manager may toss this document back,
saying words to the effect of "This is ridiculous," or "Let's stop the paperwork already. Can't you just go and find me some candidates?" It seems
like too much work to do when the hiring need is urgent.

We'll be talking much more about this situation in Chapter 9, but
if this reaction happens, you're at a moment of truth. Do you begin
down the road to hiring excellence by taking the time to think about
these fundamental questions for the job? Or do you sacrifice all that

in the interest of short-term progress? And it is only short-term; ultimately, it's costlier in time and money to hire the wrong person who isn't as productive, and may need to be replaced before long. Making an investment without a clear plan is not the way business works. Investments in people should be no different, and should receive at least as much careful thought.

Kickoff Meeting

The two key people in this meeting are the hiring manager and the recruiter. The first goal is to get alignment on what the role involves, as laid out in the Kickoff Collaboration document. Maybe the recruiter has hired lots of this type of role in the past. If that's not the case, then the hiring manager needs to spend the time going over the job in detail. Consider inviting the recruiter to your team meetings to understand where this role fits in the current team. Get the recruiter up to speed on the jargon of the job and the likely questions candidates will ask. Make sure the recruiter knows what a good hire will look like in relation to other hires you're both familiar with. The goal is to come up with an interview kit that contains all the documents needed for an interviewer to do a great job. The kit will contain materials like the internal job description, application, and résumé. But it also will contain the scorecard.

Evaluation

Once you agree on what the role involves, it's time to agree on how you're going to evaluate people for that role.

Note: The term "scorecard" is very common in the hiring community. However, it usually amounts to a lame, overall concept of "Rate this candidate on a scale from one to five." That's not far removed from "Tell me if he's any good."

A legitimately useful scorecard is much more detailed. There should be a section for technical ability, another section for culture, and yet another for soft, interpersonal skills. Within those broad labels, the scorecards will vary substantially, depending on the specific job. A Level 4 engineer's scorecard will bear only slight resemblance to the scorecard for a receptionist.

Scorecard

Below is an example of a scorecard. Typically, scorecards vary by job type.

Key take-aways

Free-form text area at the top for conclusions, pros, cons, and things to follow up on.

Focus attributes

CSS	⊗	👍	⊖	👎	☆
Communication	⊗	👍	⊖	👎	☆
Comp Sci fundamentals	⊗	👍	⊖	👎	☆
Creative	⊗	👍	⊖	👎	☆
Detail-oriented	⊗	👍	⊖	👎	☆
Focused on quality	⊗	👍	⊖	👎	☆
Total experience	⊗	👍	⊖	👎	☆
Availability	⊗	👍	⊖	👎	☆

Skills

Strong at cross-browser issues	⊗	👍	⊖	👎	☆
Strong analytical skills	⊗	👍	⊖	👎	☆

(Continued)

(Continued)

Test-driven development   ⊗ 👍 ⊖ 👎 ☆

Web architecture   ⊗ 👍 ⊖ 👎 ☆

Personality traits

Comfortable with change   ⊗ 👍 ⊖ 👎 ☆

Personable   ⊗ 👍 ⊖ 👎 ☆

Resourceful   ⊗ 👍 ⊖ 👎 ☆

Wants a startup   ⊗ 👍 ⊖ 👎 ☆

Qualifications

BA or equivalent   ⊗ 👍 ⊖ 👎 ☆

Details

Motivated for this job   ⊗ 👍 ⊖ 👎 ☆

Salary requirements   ⊗ 👍 ⊖ 👎 ☆

Overall recommendation

Definitely Not	No	Yes	Strong Yes

Please note several things about this scorecard:

- It's definitely not one-size-fits-all. This example is a technical job, so there is a clear emphasis on technical ability. Another job will look substantially different.
- The top section of Focus Attributes are the ones that this specific interviewer is supposed to focus on.
- Note how there is no 10-point scale, because such scales create meaningless distinctions between, for example, one interviewer's rating of 7 and another interviewer's rating of 8. This five-point scale is intuitive and each rating is easily distinguishable from the others.
- You're seeing a paper version of the scorecard, but an online version has the feature of including a free-form text box for each rating, so people can explain their rating. It's an essential way for people to think through the ratings they give, and you could easily create that on a spreadsheet.
- Remember that not every interviewer is rating a candidate on all elements. Just as the scorecard is customized by job, the interviewer's tasks are customized within the job. That takes pressure off a nontechnical interviewer being asked to rate cross-browser proficiency, for example.

Another way to look at these items is in three buckets: experiences, behavior traits, and skills. With experiences, you figure it out on the résumé and then verify it through a reference check. With skills, you test them by asking them to demonstrate the skills. With behavioral traits, you do behavior interviews. This is a book for leaders to reorient the basic building blocks of their hiring mechanism. We do not attempt to teach all aspects of hiring, like the ins and outs of conducting a behavioral interview.

Because we have these different dimensions on a scorecard, it is often most efficient to have different people in charge of gathering the information for particular sections. Now is the time to identify who will ask which questions and who will ensure that the appropriate testing gets done.

The result of those decisions will be an Interview Plan, as seen below.

Interview Plan

Who on the team needs to meet this person to be able to make a decision? Who are the cross-functional stakeholders who should meet this person? Let's discuss why each person is a part of the interview team.

- Application Review (Recruiter name)
- Initial Screen (Who?)
- Department Phone Interview (Who?)
- Take-Home Assignment
- Onsite Interview
  - Who? | Recruiter Tour and Demo | 15 minutes
  - Who? | Culture Interview | 45 minutes
  - Who? | Purpose? | How Long?
  - Who? | Purpose? | How Long?
  - Who? | Purpose? | How Long?
  - Who? | Purpose? | How Long?
  - Who? | Recruiter Check-In | 15 minutes
- Executive Interview | (Who?)

Ideally, you should shoot for having a candidate come in one time for all interviews. If you have a good reason to have them come in a second time, that's fine. For example, if you're a regulated industry then they may have to take a drug test. Or it could be next to impossible to have the executive interview happen on the same day. But what you want to avoid is asking the candidate to come back just because you can't seem to get all parties organized.

For each of these interviews, the recruiter then prepares the interviewers to play their role. That means making sure that they know what they're supposed to do in high definition. When they see a calendar item, they should be able to click on it and have details about the context of the job, what they need to know about the candidate, the details of the interview (who, when, where), what questions they will ask, and what their focus is.

The Kickoff Meeting Provides Important Elements for the Job Ad

The recruiter is typically responsible for writing the job ad. In Chapter 5, we discussed how there may be a job description purely for internal purposes, but what should be external-facing is the job ad. The purpose is to get applicants excited about applying for the job, and we gave some writing tips.

To the degree that the recruiter can learn in the kickoff meeting who the audience is, they can really enhance the likely performance of the ad. So, a great kickoff meeting will include questions of the hiring manager:

- Tell me about the person who you want most to respond to this ad. Who are they?
- What are they interested in?
- How do we get their attention?
- What's the hook? What's great about this job? What's unique about this job?
- What's the opportunity here for the right job seeker to get growth in this role?

That gives the recruiter enough meat to write a compelling ad. Again, it's useful to anticipate pushback from hiring managers who have not yet seen the value of a comprehensive system. They may say, "Look, I thought you're the recruiter. Go recruit me a digital marketing person, okay? Everybody knows what that means. We could use the language we used last time: 'Fast-moving, innovative company wants high-energy ninja who can think outside the box. ... '"Here is one version of what the job ad should contain:

Job ad template:

[Company] is looking for a(n) [role] to join our team!

(Description of the role, key responsibilities, reporting structure, team and/or department)

Keep it brief: 2 paragraphs max.

Who will love this job:

- Bulleted list
- Use nouns to describe the ideal candidate
- Ex: a team player, a leader, a problem-solver ...

What you'll do:

- Bulleted list
- Use verbs to describe job activities
- Ex: lead a team; motivate customers; manage processes
- Highlight team-specific activities first, then list other ways the role will interact with other teams and/or departments

You should have:

- List of qualifications
- Required qualifications first, then (if applicable) nice-to-haves
- Ex: experience building and scaling programs, comfortable delivering training and/or workshops a plus
- Your own unique talents! Even if you don't meet 100% of the qualifications outlined above, tell us why you'd be a great fit for this role in your cover letter.

One Person's Hell Is Another Person's Heaven

When we get a new customer, typically they have been storing their candidate data in one or more legacy systems. We need to help them move all that data over to our system.

Because there are countless different databases, it's often a very technical job to find that data, organize it so our system can accept it, and then migrate it to Greenhouse.

Early on, our software engineers were doing this work. Over time, with lots more customers needing the service, it became

(continued)

(*continued*)

really distracting to our engineers. In fact, they grew to dread that work. They wanted to build features!

We decided to hire a specialized data engineer to do this work. Our Chief Technical Officer (CTO) was skeptical: "That's a terrible job. In fact, it's the worst programming work we have, and we'll never find anyone good for it."

Our perspective was that there's someone out there for whom this is the best job. This is their *favorite job in the world.* Just because it's not the job the CTO wants or the engineers on our team today want, that doesn't make it a bad job. It just means it's a bad fit for the current people on the team. Let's go find the person who thinks this is their dream job.

When you take that perspective, it opens up new possibilities. How are we going to sell this job? What's good about it? We wrote a job ad that talked about the fact that every new assignment will involve detective work. Every day will bring a new challenge. And at the end of every project, you'll deliver work to a client who's really satisfied and excited that the system works so well. For the right person, that job will be amazing.

We indeed found someone who fit the job like a glove—and in fact, now we have an entire team of people doing the work.

Go Time: The Interview

The recruiter then publishes the job ad, candidates start to apply, and you put them through the process.

In Chapter 5, we talked at length about the candidate experience before and after the interview. By creating and following the interview kit we just discussed, we're ensuring that the interview itself is conducted properly. All interviewers know their roles, the questions to ask, what the schedule is, and what are the next steps. If it's a role you've done many times before, you can more or less turn the crank, do the interviews, and have people fill out the scorecards.

Filling out the Scorecards

A completed scorecard is the foundation for making a data-driven decision. *Here's what I heard and what I thought about each of the attributes. Here are my ratings, plus why I rated the person this way.*

Each person should fill out the scorecard before they speak with anyone else about the candidate and the interview. It's critical to be able to do that without the bias of first hearing what the most senior person thinks—or for that matter, what anyone else thinks. Only then should everyone be able to see how other people rated the candidate on the scorecard.

Now the scorecards get circulated and you look to see where you have consensus or disagreement. The criteria we're using were all agreed upon ahead of time, and not cooked up now. By seeing this information ahead of time, the roundup is very efficient because you can focus on the areas of disagreement that jump out from the scorecards.

As harsh as it may sound, we've found that appropriate social shaming has its place in a well-run hiring operation. By now, you clearly see that we're not saying that becoming great at hiring is easy. It's actually hard work. There is no "going through the motions" of hiring, but instead each step is intentional, important, and deserving of careful thought. That makes it at the same time hard, doable, and highly effective.

In the context of asking people to take on those deeper roles, there is no place for the slacker who will blow off scorecards, or dash them off, or show up late for hiring meetings. We will talk more about the role of the Talent Maker in Chapter 9, but part of that role is to create an environment where team players can politely but clearly get across the message of "That's not how we do things here. Stop wasting our time and start carrying your own weight."

The Roundup

Everyone who is part of the decision for this job attends the roundup. Far from being this free-for-all, people walk in knowing that the conversation is going to be focused from the outset.

For all these things that we said we were looking for, we got a whole bunch of thumbs up and thumbs down by interviewers saying this candidate has it or doesn't. It's very easy for us to see at a glance the things we all agree this person totally has. And these are the things we all agree this person does not have.

That leaves us with the things that received mixed evaluations, and they jump off the page. There may be wide disagreement about certain attributes, or one person may be consistently higher or lower than everyone else. It's these disparities that become the topics of discussion.

Organizations differ about the details on their scorecards. Some stick to the ratings only. Others want interviewers not only to do the ratings, but to give a sentence or two about why they rated the person that way. Yes, this does take extra time but we think it's a best practice. It records the basis for that person's ratings right at the time of judgment. That way, when the roundup happens and someone says, "Why did you rate the candidate so low on this attribute?" you don't have to try to recall your reasoning at the time.

So, there is a lively and maybe even heated discussion around the scorecards. But it's an efficient heat; we're not discussing the kind of person we need for the role, because that was decided in the kickoff meeting. In the roundup, we're discussing how candidates stack up against the criteria. You can start to get agreements by saying, for instance, that some of these attributes may be more important than others: This candidate is great at this one thing, and that may make up for the thing that they're bad at. Typically what you have is a bunch of imperfect people (surprise!), who don't exactly match up to everything you need in a role. So you debate about relative merits.

If it's a new role you haven't done before, there may be some iteration. After a few interviews it may become apparent that some of the questions in the interview kit didn't quite get at the attributes we were focused on. Or it could be that the attributes agreed upon at the kickoff meeting are not quite right. In either case, it's fine to make the adjustments, try them on later interviews, and see if the issues are solved.

The goal is to make each interview consistent, fair, and challenging. But we're not talking about a rigid type of consistency where we need to keep asking the same questions of all candidates, even though we want to make adjustments. Use your judgment and tune the process as little as possible, but as much as necessary for the interviews to identify the right candidates for the role.

The Interview Experience from a Diversity Perspective

It's important to think about the entire interview experience in detail, especially when you're working on increasing the diversity of your organization.

When a candidate goes to the website and looks at pictures of the people on the employee page, do they see anyone who looks like them, in terms of race, gender, or age?

Then, when they go to an interview, do they see anyone like them? Are certain people "mansplained" to much more than others?

If they're in a wheelchair and go to the office, can they get in? If they're colorblind, can they read the application? Diversity is more than just race and gender. It actually doesn't take much imagination: Look at every one of the touch points in the interview experience and think about it through the lens of diversity and belonging. It doesn't take imagination, but it does take awareness. Be intentional with the experience you create. Map out the journey somebody is going to go through.

How do you interview for a diversity mindset? To start with, you can say, "I want to hear about things you've done to build an inclusive culture in the past. I want to know about times when you went out of your way or did things that require effort or creativity in the name of including people. It could be lessons you've learned or things you've screwed up on in the past, and how you're better now because of it."

Most good interview questions are a two-way street; they not only have the benefit of helping me decide whether you're good at something, but they also tell the candidate that I care a lot about the topic.

Also keep in mind that there is a lot of utility in interviewing several people in a row, and listening closely to their answers. You'll hear answers that are head and shoulders above the others. Let's say you ask the candidate if they have created an inclusive team before. If you ask one person, it may be hard to judge the answer. But if you ask ten people in a row, it becomes much easier. What you'll hear is some people will leap at the question: "Oh, yeah, I've thought about this a ton. Okay, here's what I did and here's what I've learned. ... " It's a rich answer. Then some people will give you very generic answers along the lines of "Diversity is important to me."

When you hear somebody who's really done it, that person jumps out. This is true for diversity topics, but also for any other topic, like "Tell me about a time you've had to resolve a conflict." One person will have a short answer, and another will have a whole framework, after having dealt with the topic a bunch of times. That's one of the great benefits of structured hiring: It's so much easier to tell people apart if you ask them all the same questions.

"Are they any good?"

Daniel: I spent a decade consulting to banks. Along the way, some of my clients got to know me, and they thought I had good judgment when it came to people.

At one point, a customer of mine contacted me and said, "I'm going to be interviewing some people to hire for my team. Can you help me?" I replied, "Of course, you're my customer, and if I can help, I'd be happy to. What did you have in mind?"

She said, "Well, can you meet with this person and tell me if they're good?" That took me by surprise, coming from a senior person at this well-known bank. I said, "Um, can you elaborate a little about what you want me to do?"

"You know, I want to know if I should hire them. Tell me if they're any good. We know what good looks like, but we're just not good at this hiring stuff."

"I want to help you," I explained, "but the problem is I don't know what you are hiring this person to do, so I don't know how to judge if they're good at doing that stuff."

When I started asking questions, it seemed like it never occurred to anyone in that building to ask those things.

That was a revelation to me: *Oh my God, this hiring mess is bigger than just what I experienced at my own company.*

(continued)

(*continued*)

I realized over time that there was a whole world of people aimlessly interviewing every day. Millions of them, who never bothered to stop and ask the most basic questions about hiring, like "What should this person be good at? How will we know?"

Rubik's Cube

Daniel: In Chapter 1, I recounted how I couldn't understand why the people in my engineering company were arriving at polar opposite conclusions about the same candidate they interviewed.

Many things became clear to me once I was able to listen to recordings of the interviews. For example, that's how I found out about the Rubik's Cube question one of my guys liked to ask.

He reported to me in the strongest terms that the recent candidate he interviewed would be a bad fit for our company. It turned out that he had a favorite interview question that he had asked over the course of his career: Imagine that you took apart a Rubik's Cube and you dropped all the parts all in a bucket of red paint. How many little surfaces would be covered in red? Apparently the candidate did a terrible job on that question.

I thought, "Wait, why are we asking that question? What does that have to do with the job?" My interviewer was puzzled at me—it was completely self-evident to him that we shouldn't hire any person who could not answer that brain teaser.

And so it led down this whole path of let's try to ask only questions that are directly helping us decide whether the person is good at the job.

Google made famous a whole category of interview questions, stuff like "You've been reduced to the size of a nickel and dropped in a blender. How would you escape?" or "How many golf balls would fit in a 747?" They asked these sorts of questions

(*continued*)

(*continued*)

for years. Finally, they did the research and realized that answering the questions had zero predictive power of success at Google. It was just a giant waste of everyone's time at best, and likely also contributed to bias.

That reinforced to me the principle of making sure you ask questions that have relevance for the role. It's fine to test for specific skills, but no puzzles are necessary.

Good Decision-Making Is No Guarantee

We did not write this book with the premise that if you follow our formula, you'll never have a bad hire. We also are not claiming that we've somehow reached enlightenment where we have all the answers and only make purely rational decisions. We're all in this together, moving along the path of getting better at hiring. There will always be subjective elements, and that's part of being a leader.

Our goal is to help you do a few things. First, to make confident decisions that are based on more evidence and less bias. Second, to have a better overall hiring experience for everyone involved. And third, to be able to move faster through the process.

You'll also have more confidence in the decisions that you make, so you can act with more conviction on them. For example, we talked in Chapter 2 about a situation when a candidate counteroffers or says they have another job. Using the data that you've collected from a good structured process, you can negotiate more effectively.

We're pretty sure that great hiring can never reach the stage of paint-by-number, automatic mechanisms. Instead, what we're after are effective, repeatable systems that deliver the facts on which you can make solid judgments.

Note

1. https://bit.ly/2YTRQhB.

Chapter 7: Takeaways

An important aspect of structured hiring is to create an environment where higher-quality, informed decisions can be made. That involves several things.

We all have biases; it's part of being human. One of those biases is the **tendency to favor people who are like us**, or who share certain experiences with us like college, sports, and so on.

Other common biases are to be **influenced by what the most senior person thinks**, what we think they want to hear, or what the majority of the group thinks. There are many more.

The goal is to minimize them by **following a systematic approach when making decisions**; it's also to make every interview consistent, fair, and challenging.

A robust hiring process includes **kickoff collaboration, the kickoff meeting, an interview plan, and a data-driven roundup.**

When asking questions about inclusive cultures or other diversity topics, **pay attention to the level of detail you're hearing**, versus statements like "Yes, that's important to me."

Good decision-making is no guarantee, but it helps to create a **fair and effective** basis for hiring the best people.

Expert Insights: Beth Steinberg

Please tell us a bit about your background.

I was in people and talent during a very fast growth period for Nordstrom. During my 12 years there, we hired in excess of 10,000 employees.

Then I went into the world of tech in a variety of emerging companies and more established companies like Facebook, Nike, and Electronic Arts, as well as a number of fast-growing companies like Sunrun, BrightRoll, and Chime.

Wherever I am, I try to bring some of that maturity around planning around talent, thinking about it as a strategic imperative, and focusing on the things you need to do to equip yourself for the next three to five years.

What's your promise to the CEO?

My number one promise that I make myself and the CEO is that wherever we end up, we don't want to lose what made us special at the beginning—we're still a culture that we're proud of and want to be a part of.

You hear about a lot of companies where you get to that stage of going public or being large and they're like "Who are we? Who have we turned into?" My promise is that we can maintain our culture and values if we focus on whom we hire, and what we do with people once we hire them.

What do you ask of the CEO?

What I ask of the CEO is that they understand that the only way they'll be successful in hiring is if they have commitment and partnership. The talent team creates the process, the systems, and finds the candidate, but this is not a function of just that team.

I really learned that in the early days of Facebook, where I worked with Mark Zuckerberg. When I first started working for him, he was probably 22. He understood that hiring was a team sport, and that everybody had to be committed to it. So, I ask CEOs to make sure they are committed to talent acquisition and to reinforce that their people need to be engaged in this also. It is absolutely critical to the process.

Can you think of a situation where the CEO was committed, but you had to do a lot of work with individual leaders who weren't quite on that same page?

The transformation happened when those leaders saw that they could not produce their commitments to the company. Because they didn't have the right people and they hadn't hired appropriately, they couldn't achieve their objectives.

The reality is we hire people to make the company successful. The turnaround happens when a leader will say: "Where did we go wrong here? How do we start looking at the capabilities and competencies we need, and where do we find that talent?" It's a huge evolution from thinking, "Oh, I like this person; let's hire this person."

Sometimes, the hiring manager thinks the problem is the recruiting team. It's hard for them to realize that the problem is they themselves are not participating effectively. What would you put in place where there's visibility and transparency on everything that's happening on both sides of the equation?

I have a situation like that right now. The product team's saying, "You guys don't find the right people." We're saying, "You're not at all engaged in the process."

The solution is to get alignment and clarity on *what is the process* and why that process exists. You have to think strategically about competencies and share pipeline data. We also show a lot of pipeline data to everybody. That's because everybody blames the pipeline: *If you only found more candidates, the problem would be solved.*

I recently had a situation where I could show that we had plenty of people at the top of the funnel, but conversions were the problem. We were not converting people after the first interview to the second interview; therefore, we were not achieving what we needed to achieve. It's crucial to have the data, so you can break it down and find the actual root problem.

How do you balance the need to fight today's fires—getting interviews scheduled, offers out, and roles filled—with stepping back and working on systems and tools such that you'll get to where you need to be over the next two years?

What you need are solid strategic leaders underneath the head of talent, so that person can get some headspace to think about long-term things. Long-term talent planning and development planning is very hard to do in fast-moving companies because it requires you to stop and do what I call "slow thinking" instead of fast thinking. You need to really plot out where you see your company going in two to three years and work backwards from there.

You need to look externally for the talent and the competencies that you lack. But you also need to be able to assess talent internally and be able to develop people internally. You must have enough balance between strategic and tactical tasks to create the space to make that happen. It's hard. It's really a new muscle that leaders need to develop. For many years, it was all about butts in seats, but that's not the game anymore.

Talent is a long game, not a short game. If you play the short game, you're going to get short-game results. If you want to be an enduring company, you must play the long game.

What are other mistakes you see companies make?

A lot of people try to fix every ill with a body. I have a model where I talk about culture, structure, talent management, systems, and process.

Good companies don't solve problems with a body, unless they actually have figured out what they're trying to solve.

If you have a structural issue where there are no clear goals, roles, and alignment, you can hire as many people as you want but it won't solve the problem; in fact, it will create more problems. That's what I'm talking about around "slow thinking." You need the credibility to say, "Let's take a step back. What are we solving for, and why? Are we going to get there by hiring this position? Or is there something more systemic going on that we need to deal with first?"

It's a discipline, and it is very hard to do because you have a lot of pressure. The common metric that is used for success is "We've doubled in size," or whatever. That can be a meaningless metric, but we're so used to having that be a metric of success. It might instead be a metric of laziness and lack of strategy.

How do you think leaders should be thinking about recruiting operations?

That's interesting, because many companies don't even have a recruiting operations team, never mind a sophisticated one. I would recommend that emerging companies put that in sooner rather than later. You need to have somebody who thinks day in and day out about the process, the candidate experience, the hiring brand, and how that is currently working. What sources are currently working out the best for you, based on hard data. I believe that role should be hired almost in tandem with a talent leader. That way you can start building those capabilities, so you can show people a different way of doing it, because talent is really a process.

You get approached by a lot of folks who'll say, "Come help figure us out," and you have to diagnose where they are. From an operational excellence perspective, what do you do to figure out where they're at?

The first thing I usually do is talk to the leaders to see how they're oriented around talent. Do they think that they have skin in this game or not? You can tell a lot by those conversations. If they're spending fewer than 10 percent of their time on talent, or if they don't look at the metrics or even know the metrics, then I have to ask, "How committed are you to this? What do you see your role in this?"

I often see a lot of company-wide celebrations when things go well and a lot of blaming the talent team when things don't go well. That's not fair, and it won't help you to solve the problem. One thing I'm working on now is to take data from different sources and do an internal scorecard, rating leaders. It looks at leadership effectiveness in terms of engagement in hiring, employee engagement data, turnover data, and so on. It's not done as a punitive measure, but to say this is where we need to help you succeed.

I think we do a disservice to people by assuming that they know how to hire effectively. Why would we assume that? I mean, I could be an engineer, but I would need to study for it and practice it. With leadership, we do not treat it like a skill and a competency that needs training and practice. I truly believe that's why a lot of things go bad in companies.

Let's say a leader reads this book and wants to develop a well-honed talent operation. How would you summarize what needs to be in place?

Do you have repeatable systems and processes in place? Are you balancing short term with long term? Are you proud of the process? If you went through the process would you think, *Wow, I want to join this company!*

Are you developing relationships to be a good partner around talent? Are you really creating the relationships with your recruiting coordinators, sourcers, and recruiters, in order to make sure that they understand what your expectations are?

You're doing yourself, your team, and the company a disservice if you are not operating as well as you should in those areas. Of course, you're going to have fits and starts where things go well and maybe they get off track, but do you have the relationships so you can always get things back on track?

Expert Insights: Tope Awotona

Babatope (Tope) Awotona is the founder and CEO of Calendly, a beautiful, simple scheduling tool that in less than five years has served close to 30 million people worldwide. Tope was born in Lagos, Nigeria, moved to America in high school, and became an entrepreneur after a successful career in software at companies like IBM and EMC.

We know you get very personally involved with hiring at Calendly. Could you please describe how that breaks down in terms of time spent?

In the past year, 75 percent of my hiring involvement was on hiring my executive team; about 20 percent was spent hiring VPs and senior managers reporting to those folks, and the final 5 percent was elsewhere.

What does it look like when you get involved with hiring when it's not potentially one of your direct reports?

It runs the gamut and it's everything from their presenting a 90-day plan to me, to spending time with them to understand their leadership and team-building philosophy. The most exciting is when I get to share the company vision and connect it to their role. One of our teams was trying to hire an individual contributor. This person was really talented and had another offer. The team asked if I was willing to make a video to help convince the candidate to take our offer, and of course, I said yes.

It was a pretty simple video, actually. I told the candidate how important the role was. I then went through the things that they would be specifically working on, and how excited I was at the prospect of their joining the team, and how they could help us to have a great year next year and beyond.

It's really important to put yourself in the shoes of the candidate. If you're hiring great talent, you can bet they're vetting you thoroughly. They're good, they're highly coveted, and they know it. Even if you pay really well, you won't always be able to differentiate just on the compensation. It becomes important to appeal to the universal need for growth and development. They often can matter just as much as all the other benefits.

So, back to the competitive candidate: We did our homework about what this person cared about, and I helped the team to make the best pitch we could. The person signed with us.

When you think about the journey you've been on from founding the company until now, has your view of the importance of hiring stayed fairly constant or has it changed?

It's changed. Just today, I had a call with a leader who joined our company this week. When I think back to my approach a couple of years ago, the conversation today would have been mostly about catching this person up on learning about the business, and that certainly is important. But instead our entire conversation today was about hiring. For all my direct reports, hiring is a recurring Objectives and Key Results (OKRs) each quarter.

We've heard you talk about the leverage that your next group of hires will have compared with your personal leverage. Could you elaborate on that?

I look at it as a mathematical thing. When you're the founder and the company is small, then it's natural for people to involve you in lots of decisions, along the lines of "What does Tope think about this?" or "I wonder if Tope will like this approach." Maybe that worked when we were a 20-person company. But now that we have hundreds of employees, and as a human being I represent just a fraction of one percent of the company. Sure, I have influence as the founder, but even so, I can't be in all the conversations. I cannot possibly be talking with as many of our customers as all the people we hire are doing. So, the simple math is that the people we hire end up doing the bulk of the work that gets done.

When you look at things from a mathematical standpoint, it shapes how you view the importance of hiring, and also the importance of making sure that your people are successful and happy in their jobs.

How do you view the leader's role in the earlier planning phases like job descriptions?

One thing I pay particular attention to is whether job descriptions reflect what we actually need. Certain events in a business create the need for a role. Then when someone writes a job description, there's often a certain drift or difference between the events and that job description. Then when you interview people, any individual presents a set of skills that can deviate even more from the job description. One thing I've found to be important is to make sure that the end result of whom we hire does not drift too much from the original need.

Of course, people vary and roles change, and that's part of business. But I think one function of a leader is to keep an eye on the direction we're moving with the business and with finding talent, to make sure that they're aligned and that we make any changes deliberately instead of through unintentional drift.

Also if a role is pretty senior and we've never hired for it before, I'll put more of my focus there. I'll participate in the interview panel. I focus a great deal on the exercises that we have candidates go through. I'll spend 45 minutes with them, having them present their exercise, and digging into their thought processes. What I'm really trying to understand is how much original thinking went into their answer. How much do they understand the particular challenge, and can they defend their approach to it? Lots of people are good at handling interview questions, so I like to focus more on these exercises as a way of understanding a candidate better.

Another thing I do sounds simple, but you'd be surprised: I ask them to describe the role. I say, "Forget about the job description; you've been through a number of interviews, so you've heard a lot of things. In your own words, how would you describe the role?" As with my comment earlier about job descriptions, here too it's a matter of getting alignment of expectations on both sides.

Early on I heard many interesting answers. Sometimes, people wanted to land the stellar candidate so much that they ended up telling them things that either were not true, or that might not happen for several years—things like an individual contributor could become a manager or director in six months. So, 90 percent of what I do there is to make sure that the expectations are aligned with ours about their role and their opportunities for growth within the company. Those expectation misalignments don't happen very often now, given that we have more rigor in our hiring processes.

8

Driving Operational Excellence

If you're familiar with software development, then you know about systems like Agile. They are frameworks for collaborating, where— among other things— you get together regularly, look back at the work recently done, and collectively think, *How can we do this better?*

The same is certainly true of sales organizations. The good ones do a lot of planning, have debriefs, and even hire sales-enablement experts to train people how to sell better.

Yet how many organizations put an equivalent emphasis on improving the hiring process? Well, when you're through with this chapter, you'll know how to put a crucial part of the system in place to do just that, and why it's so important.

First Class All the Way

Organizations that are great at hiring have made hiring a first-class process that deserves continual attention. It's a massive evolution compared with the organizations that relegate hiring to something they occasionally pull out and then store away, like the company punchbowl.

Getting great at hiring means building processes with clear key performance indicators (KPIs) and measuring with the intention of continuous improvement. This is the competency that we call "Use data to drive operational excellence and improve over time." It's a little different from the other three competencies—the candidate experience, recruiting, and making hiring decisions. This fourth competency is the thread to weave those other three into the fabric of your organization.

That thread is made of data: How can you use data to measure and improve all the elements of the hiring experience?

For example, let's say you want to improve diversity. If you don't know where the problems are—really know, versus just having a hunch—then you might say, "We need to post our jobs at historically black colleges." That might be fine, except the data might show that you have enough candidates from underrepresented groups in the top of your funnel already. The problem may be happening during the first or subsequent interviews. It's about using data to find and fix the right problem.

The Component Parts

As we said, data is at the core of this competency, but so are measuring, auditing, and designing intentionally.

Measuring. Strictly speaking, the data is not always that interesting. When you combine, parse, and filter the data so you can see trends and anomalies—that's where it becomes useful information and insights.

Auditing. The old adage recommends that you "trust, but verify." We don't use the term "auditing" to suggest that you hire more accountants to review the books. We mean that you need to know what's actually going on inside processes and conversations.

One way to audit is what I (Daniel) did a million years ago when I was trying to figure out why my two interviewers arrived at polar opposite conclusions about whether we should hire someone. I described in Chapter 1 how I listened to recordings of the interviews and instantly found the cause—something that would never have made it into a report.

Another way to audit is to invite feedback. We've (fortunately) only had a very few occasions when employees wanted to talk with one of us about how they were treated in the company. On the one hand, we were shocked to hear what a manager thought was appropriate; on the other hand, we were grateful that people felt safe in bringing this behavior to our attention. We swiftly took care of the problem.

Designing intentionally. You've seen this principle in action in earlier chapters. You don't leave important, frequent processes like interviewing to chance. They should not only be scripted, but scrutinized, so the granular experience is something you can be proud of. The same is true for rejection letters, offers, surveys, and other communications. But it does not stop with communications; it extends to how visible you make hiring as a primary strategic function in your organization. More on that in Chapter 9.

Problem Signs

Let's look at three symptoms that indicate there's work to be done in order to become operationally strong.

1. **Systems and tools do not mesh.** When somebody is building a whole recruiting function, they don't just buy an Applicant Tracking System (ATS). They buy a whole bunch of specialist tools, and these in turn need to plug into a wider IT infrastructure.

   In a company that's operating chaotically, all of those different tools don't natively talk to each other, nor is effort made to integrate them. If you hire somebody in the ATS, then you must retype all their information over in some HR system. Then if you want to do a video interview, you go to the ATS, pull the candidate's name out, go into the video interview system, type in the name, and hit send.

   As we talked about in Chapter 2, this situation may not even be met with much conscious frustration; it's just the way all systems "work" in the organization, and in the ones people worked at previously. It's just life. The occasional suggestion to have the systems talk with each other is usually met by a combination of "That's easy for you to say—it's a nightmare to pull it off," "I'd love to but we don't have the budget or time," or the tried-and-true "We'll put that on the dev list. It's a pretty long list, you know."

It may be a long list, but having a long list of excuses to bat away the suggestion is evidence of where priorities lay.

2. **People don't live in the tools.** Let's say HR and IT have worked hard to buy systems that talk with each other, or they built those linkages. Without effective training and enforcement in place, people will drift away from those systems and keep their own private information on Excel spreadsheets, Google Sheets, and many other tools, including on paper. "It's just easier that way," they say. "I have my own system and it works for me." You can see this attitude in sticky notes everywhere, people sending spreadsheet attachments, and taking paper notes.

Of course, this becomes a vicious cycle: If the system has no useful information, then no one relies on it, or updates it.

Daniel: I was pitching a prospective customer a while back. It was a 600-person global advertising agency. I was trying to make the business case for software: "You know, maybe one way you could profit from buying Greenhouse is by reducing your need for agency spend. You guys are probably using a lot of staffing agencies, given your size. If you had a system that allowed you to do some of your own recruiting and sourcing, it might more than pay for our software. Plus, it could help you to build an even stronger hiring brand. How much do you spend on recruiting agencies?"

The head of recruiting said, "I have no idea."

I'm like, "Wait. What?"

"I have no clue, Daniel. We've no record of it anywhere."

I rolled up my sleeves and gave him some ideas of where to look. We did some math on a notepad, and it turned out they were spending around $3 million a year on it.

Now both of us were shocked. He said that he knew *how* it happened, but just didn't know the magnitude. He explained, "Our advertising agency pitches big clients all the time. They don't involve me as head of recruiting. It's the CD Creative Director (CD) and the head of business development who do the pitching.

"So, what they'll do is pitch some big airline, and win the deal. Great news—except now they need to get a 25-person creative team spun up in Chicago for this client in 14 days. They have zero expectation that recruiting or HR can solve that problem for them. And so all they know is they have a big check coming from the customer and a lot of work to do—fast. So, they call up an agency or two and say, 'I'm gonna need 20 creatives on site in Chicago as fast as you can. Start sending résumés.' They pay a 30 percent contingency fee of the first-year salary of each of those new hires. It all comes out of the project budget. And that's just for the one project. We're a worldwide agency."

In organizations like this, there are no higher-level discussions taking place, like arguing whether we should be measuring time-to-hire versus time-to-fill. There are no measurements. There is no measuring tape, and even if there were, there's no time.

In fact, we'll mention certain common reports to people in companies of shockingly large size, who will tell us, "We literally don't get any of the reports you just mentioned. And the reports we do get, we don't believe." We'll say, "So, what are you going to get better at next quarter? If you look at this whole practice of hiring and all the things you're doing, how do you project that you'll be doing them differently versus how you do them today?" They squint and look at you like you have three heads.

"So, how could the head of recruiting begin to get their hands around what's happening in the organization?"

One good way is to focus on the approval process. When you open a job, who approves it? Where is the record of that? Has someone from accounting signed off? How about the hiring manager? Organizations will vary widely in this regard, but it's a starting place to get a handle on the activity actually happening in this opaque environment. We'll discuss this more in Chapter 10.

3. **Too much red tape.** This happens to stodgy organizations that have become overly process-driven. You can't get anything done because of all the red tape.

> *Daniel:* We hosted a dinner one time for recruiting and HR leaders, and I was talking to this person about how to create a great job posting. I said it's actually a job ad, where you want to put stuff in there that's really going to sing. It will make people excited and the right person will be attracted to the ad.

She was like, "Yeah, Legal wouldn't ever let us do that." I looked puzzled. "Oh, I'm serious," she said. "There's all this regulation and so we have to say, you know, 27 paragraphs in all of our job postings about blah, blah, blah." I've been around a whole lot of attorneys in my time and I was scratching my head. "Um, what regulations are those, exactly?" She answered, "Look, I don't know. That's not my job. All I know is it will never happen here."

It's like the situation I mentioned in Chapter 1 with the head of derivatives trading at a major firm. He wanted to hire someone, filled out a bunch of forms and sent them to Cincinnati, and it took forever to hear anything back. This indicates a failure mode of overprocessing that's just as bad as the opposite.

Reading the Riot Act

Patty McCord was famously the Chief People Officer at Netflix. She wrote a culture manifesto that became quite well-known in HR circles and in Silicon Valley. She told this story that happened during the Netflix rise. At one of our events, she explained how her recruiters were demanding operational excellence from the business side. However, one of the hiring managers was pushing back. The recruiter was explaining what they needed in order to work effectively with the business side—about how you need to make a plan and automate certain things.

The manager was like, "No, I'm not doing all that. You have to just find my person now."

The recruiter said, "Listen, this is the service we provide. If you think you can do a better job hiring on your own without our service, God bless you. You're welcome to. But if you want our hiring power, you do it the way we outline it."

That story illustrates that there is a control point on hiring that companies sometimes overlook: Managers want to make their hires. You can put in place a sort of check and balance and empower the recruiting team, and you tell them that it's part of their job to hold the business side accountable. Then the hiring manager literally cannot post a job on the careers page without recruiting approving the job and pushing the button. That's a powerful checkpoint.

We will be talking at greater length in Chapter 9 about methods of effecting change. However, it's relevant to explain here how we would go about getting accurate reports when people are not living in the tools, and data does not flow seamlessly between systems.

As a leader, you need to start to demand data: "There are some reports I want to see at the end of every month. One of the reports is "For the people we hired, where did we find them?" When you see that you made 10 agency hires, you can do the math and realize that you just spent $250,000.

So, what happens is first you say, "I need to see this data and understand where we got the candidates we're getting, how many candidates we're getting, and what hires we're making." The recruiting team says, "We don't have all that data that cleanly," or "It's gonna be really manual," or "Nobody puts that stuff in this system." You go, "Uh huh, right. That's the data I need to see. I'm going to judge your success based on that data. And I want the current report to be emailed out every week." They'll say, "Don't email that! It's all wrong! It doesn't reflect reality at all," to which you then reply, "That's your problem—not anybody else's problem." "

This is because when you see companies that have no data and nothing's in the system, how do you judge if the recruiter is doing a good job? You can't. It's then effectively based on just rumors.

If there's something really important that you want done, make it someone's job. So if you think that building operational excellence in recruiting is important, have somebody be in charge of that.

Useful Measurements for Hiring

Businesses in the business-to-business (B2B) space are familiar with a marketing and sales funnel that looks like Figure 8.1.

The measurements that are based on these stages of the funnel allow the organization to set goals and judge progress toward them.

Figure 8.1   The Well-Known B2B Sales Funnel.

A similar structure exists in recruiting, as shown in Figure 8.2.

Figure 8.2   Why Not Measure Recruiting in a Similarly Rigorous Way?

At a minimum, an organization should be tracking five key performance indicators (KPIs) that relate to recruiting:

1. **Qualified candidates per opening.** This is the recruiting version of a "marketing qualified lead," A KPI would not be raw numbers of candidates, because sources like certain job boards can deliver huge

numbers of candidates that are quickly disqualified. A "qualified candidate" is judged to have sufficient skills and experience to merit a screening call.

One good measurement leads to another: Once you have the overall number of qualified candidates per opening, it's logical to want to know which sources are most effective in generating those candidates.

In addition, once you gather enough data over time on qualified candidates per opening, you can look at it per role. That allows you to determine the average number of candidates you're likely to need in order to fill a role. You'll then have an internal benchmark to know how soon you're likely to fill a role. Although roles differ widely, in general we like to generate 15–20 qualified candidates per open role.

2. **Candidate survey results.** We discussed the candidate experience at length in Chapter 5. The candidate experience is a leading indicator of the speed that a role may be filled. For every candidate who's offered a job, many more do not get an offer—but both kinds of candidates may well tell their positive or negative story on Glassdoor. That in turn has a significant effect on your hiring brand. Your sourcing activities may generate awareness of open roles, but it's your hiring brand strength that partly determines how many of those aware people become applicants.

   If your survey results are strong and improving over time, then more power to you. But if the number is trending down—or steady but low—consider it a warning. Look at the individual ratings within the surveys to see what the problem spots are. Aggregate numbers are convenient but sometimes mask what's going on, so be sure to slice the surveys by department. You may find that an average number is masking some quite poor performers who are being offset by some strong performers.

3. **Source to close.** This is how quickly candidates move through your recruiting and interview process. It's the number of days between when a candidate applies and when their offer is resolved, by being either accepted or rejected. To give you some sense of magnitude, the average source to close for Greenhouse customer organizations is 39 days.

4. **Offer acceptance rate.** This is the percentage of offers extended to candidates who are accepted. Your hiring brand definitely can affect your acceptance rate. But an equally important factor is the candidate experience. That ordeal is so bad at so many organizations that even a minimal effort at improving the experience can yield positive results. As we also discussed in Chapter 5, there's no reason why you can't significantly improve your offer acceptance rates by mapping and improving the dozens of micro-impressions you make on applicants, as they become candidates and possibly employees.

When you track both the offer acceptance rate and candidate survey results, you can get more of a sense of cause and effect. For example, you might see a downtrend in both survey comments about "The salary I was offered was competitive" and lower offer acceptance rates. It's important to not confuse anecdotal evidence with statistically significant trends, but if you do have a strong trend, it can help to guide your efforts toward improvements that actually make a difference.

5. **Hires to goal.** This KPI is the big-picture outcome of your hiring efforts in a given period. You should be establishing your hiring goal by month, quarter, and year. The goal should not be some arbitrary challenge on the part of a leader, but instead the result of knowing your numbers: how long it historically takes for you to fill your funnel with quality applicants, move them through the process, and close offers.

When you assess how you did against your hiring goal, slice the numbers by department: Is one of them significantly lagging the others? Has it been the case for several reporting periods? Is that problem evident in the "qualified candidates per opening" number? Or is that okay, but offer acceptance rates are unusually low?

Just step back for a moment and think about the quality of the conversations when a leadership team has the data for these KPIs, and is not flying blind. It's hard enough to do all the things that it takes to run a great organization when you have a full set of measurements to guide your way. But once you do have those measurements, it seems insane to think that you can operate an organization without them. How can you possibly make intelligent decisions without them about what's broken or working, what actions to take, and were those actions effective? Just these handful of KPIs, when diligently tracked, can become a powerful navigational guide for you.

Another Important Measurement: Quantity versus Quality of Sources

You see one version of this chart in Figure 8.3.

Quantity is measured by the number of applicants per job across the organization in a given period. Quality is measured by how far candidates got in the pipeline.

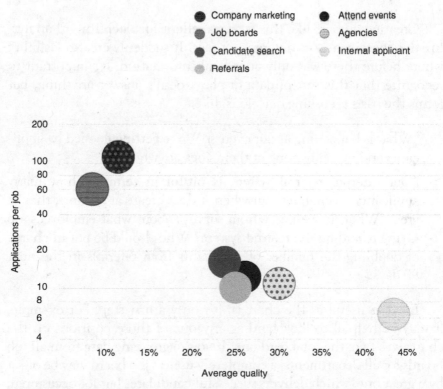

Figure 8.3   One Way to Think about Sourcing Success.

There is no industry standard for what the quality percentages represent, and the granularity will depend on the steps in your hiring funnel. Here is one example:

0 percent = Rejected immediately

10 percent = Passed initial application review

20 percent = Passed detailed application review

35 percent = Passed phone screen

50 percent = Passed first interview round

65 percent = Passed test administration

80 percent = Passed second interview round

90 percent = Passed reference check

100 percent = Received an offer

Creating a chart like this is an excellent first step toward analyzing the effectiveness of different sources. It suddenly creates visibility where before there was only anecdotal information. It's important to recognize that this sort of data display doesn't answer anything, but forms the basis for asking questions, like:

"What is happening at our events? We're getting flooded by applicants and virtually none of them goes anywhere."

"Our internal referral system is pitiful in terms of how many applicants it generates, but when it does create applicants, they're great. What do we know from surveys about what employees are saying regarding the referral system? Who should be put in charge of doubling the number of applicants from referrals in the next 90 days?"

Even as useful as the chart is, it's only a first step. For example, it may be helpful to look hard at any one of those positions on the chart; let's take the job board one. If you're grouping data from all job boards for all departments, a completely useless job board may be offset by a great one, which delivers successful candidates but for occasional, specialized roles.

In addition, is there seasonality in the numbers, where some sources are much more or less effective during the course of a year? Do some offices experience radically different outcomes than others? This is all to say that the averages are a great place to begin to ask questions. Then it takes much more analysis to arrive at some answers.

Just think for a moment if you had a regular system that collected all these data points, and presented findings all the way from big-picture averages and trends, down to granular results and insights. Then in turn those discussions would lead to hypotheses to test in the next period, about doubling down on certain sources and dropping others.

"Yeah sure. Maybe in your organization that's possible, but not in mine. We're lucky to have any data at all."

That may be the case at the moment. We're not suggesting that you need to hire staffs of rocket scientists with vast computer resources. What we are suggesting to you, as a leader, is there is nothing stopping you from getting better at collecting data and analyzing it. You don't need more than junior high school mathematics to do the analysis, which can be done in a free, online spreadsheet.

There is, however, one unusual asset that you'll need and without it, this analysis won't happen. It's your desire to make the time, despite all the time pressures and other priorities, to begin the process of collecting and analyzing more data. It will never be the most urgent thing you have to do on any given day. But if you steadily move the effort along, pretty soon you'll be able to harvest the insights that will be there for the taking.

The Time-Lapse Evolution of Hyper-Growth Companies

We've worked with lots of companies that have skyrocketed to become household names. They went from start-up to multi-billion-dollar valuation in very short order. You can see their names on our website.

In the big picture, not many companies in the world grow this fast. They basically have infinite money and are super famous. Everyone wants to work there. So, on the one hand, boo-hoo when you hear they have problems. On the other hand, we call this the "time-lapse evolution" because it's like these companies experience an organizational lifetime of issues—they just do it in three or four years

There are some good takeaways from seeing how normal issues and forces get magnified 10,000X in these situations—and how to navigate successfully through that craziness.

There may be many different flavors of hyper-growth companies, but in our experience, certain common patterns and pitfalls emerge:

- The extreme need for hiring talent puts huge pressures on recruiters, regardless of the budget they have to work with. The result is high recruiter turnover, which leads to little operational continuity.
- Organizational maturity lags behind the organization's scale and scope—often by a lot.
- Some people who have been with the company since the early days keep getting promoted. The result is junior people in leadership positions.
- The recruiting-operations office is way behind from a structural perspective. Given the company size, it should have a four-person recruiting operations team and it has zero.
- There is a focus on filling seats at the expense of everything else.
- They can get lots of candidates and they can underpay. People take the jobs because they want to work at a sexy company, and that masks a lot of problems.
- Somebody turns down a job because the company did a terrible job of interviewing them. It doesn't matter, because there's somebody behind them who wants the job. So, they get away with that until it utterly cracks.
- Practices that are followed at headquarters don't leave the building, so every other office invents their own thing from scratch.
- As soon as they start to try to go public, the company runs up against a ton of compliance and governance issues. The lack of process that was fine as a start-up now becomes a huge weakness.
- If these companies had an ATS at all, it's something that they configured for a 50-person company. They're now a 5,000-person company and are trying to use it the same way. So, they think it's busted and begin to live outside the tool.

Because the company is so high profile, they get a ton of inbound applicants effortlessly, and this masks the underlying problems. For a while, they can kind of get away with it. Poor candidate experience, no proactive sourcing, and low offer-acceptance rates can be swept under the rug as long as tons of people are spontaneously applying.

What It Looks Like When Things Start to Crack

- There's no useful data, because they didn't need it before. Recruiting results are unpredictable and hard to improve.
- Processes start to break. Manual processes that were okay at a smaller scale are no longer feasible.
- Culture is compromised in the rush to fill seats. That leads to increased attrition and the word soon gets out about what it's *really* like to work there.
- Inconsistency has grown across departments and offices. As a result, there are different cultures and different outcomes.
- When it's time to go global or become a government contractor, compliance becomes a giant blocker.
- The senior people who are there are like, "I've been here since we were 50 people and this is how we've always done it." Those people have to go, and that's really painful because they're usually cultural pillars by virtue of having been there for so long.
- Decision making gets muddled. There is a lack of experienced leadership—of people who can see the future because they've been there before. That leads to irrational decisions, or no decisions.
- Sometimes the situation gets so bad that the company effectively needs to start over.

'A Repeating Pattern at Hyper-Growth Companies

Here are some recommendations for such organizations. Ensure your head of talent acquisition (TA) has seen the scale you'll be in 12–24 months. When you go from 50 people to 1,000 people and the person is like, "Wow, I'm struggling to keep up!" that's a bad sign. You're going to be 5,000 people in 24 months, and this person is hopelessly overwhelmed at 1,000? You need somebody who's been there and thus can see around the corners.

You need to build a recruiting ops team that knows backward and forward the four main aspects of operational rigor:

1. Data governance. Ensure that clean data is collected.
2. Consistent processes. Ensure that one way is followed across all offices.
3. Proactive transparency. Produce regular reports for all levels of the organization: executive, hiring manager, and recruiter performance management.
4. Technology and automation. Have specific responsibility for all TA systems and integrations.

Even though this is a chapter about operations, we're going to save a more detailed discussion of recruiting operations for Chapter 10. The function involves authority and influence, and is central to what a leader—a Talent Maker—needs to put in place for an organization to be great at hiring.

Chapter 8: Takeaways

Operational excellence comes from making hiring a first-class process that's focused on by leaders, is continually improved upon, and consists of measuring, auditing, and designing intentionally.

Symptoms of poor processes include the following:

- **Systems and tools do not mesh** when everyone does their own thing. Data is duplicated, it's hard to know which versions of documents are the latest, and reporting is a nightmare.
- **People don't live in the central tools.** This may be due to people having their favorite spreadsheets, or not having been trained on the central tools. Either way, it becomes a downward spiral until people commit to using one central set of tools.
- **Too much red tape.** Identify where hiring processes slow to a crawl, which is problematic for candidates and employees alike. Make it someone's job to get consensus and begin to streamline those processes.

Of the dozens of possible measures of hiring performance, here are some of the most useful ones: useful hiring measurements

- **Qualified candidates per opening** gives you an internal benchmark for how soon you're likely to fill a role. It's more useful if you don't have just an overall average, but instead calculate it separately by role.

- **Candidate survey results** are a critical measurement of your brand reputation. Be sure to measure continuously and by department, with departments rewarded or held responsible for results, as the case may be.
- **Source to close** tells you how quickly or slowly candidates move through your hiring process. Improving this number can pay dividends in a better candidate experience, and a more competitive hiring brand.
- **Offer acceptance rate** is one of the better measures of your hiring brand and candidate experience. It merits regular monitoring.
- **Hires to goal** gives you the big-picture outcome of your hiring efforts in a given period. As with other measures, it's best done not only in aggregate but also by department.
- **Quality versus quantity by source** allows your hiring dollars to go much farther, because you'll be able to make informed decisions about the sources that actually produce results for you.

Expert Insights: Pattie Money

Pattie Money was former Chief People Officer at Twilio, former CPO at Sendgrid, and currently a member of the Board of Advisors of the University of Colorado Denver Business School. She has over 25 years of HR leadership experience.

When you think about the best leaders you've worked with, how do they judge the business value of hiring great talent?

For most of the people who do this incredibly well, they're super intentional because the cost of getting it wrong is so high. What does the mistaken hire cost your team? What does it cost your company? What does it cost you as a leader in your credibility? That's a lot of downside.

Do any examples come to mind?

I had an SVP of engineering who needed to hire a VP. Things were urgent, the scale of the business had gotten too big too quickly, they needed help desperately, and they made a hire that, although qualified, they were unsure of in terms of how they would lead the team.

The person was a bad hire, and after three months they were gone. But just in that short period the person had done considerable damage—especially to the credibility of the SVP with the team, not to mention also losing a couple of great people because of it.

As a result, the next time around the SVP was much more intentional in their hiring process: a ton of situational interviewing, bringing the person through a number of scenarios, and also dinner and lunch. I think the poor candidate went through 11 interviews before we finally made that hire. But by the time we were ready to get married, so to speak, everyone was confident that this was going to be a great fit, and it was. Here's the thing: The second time around, the urgency was still there. They desperately needed this hire. But the urgency did not change the importance of getting the hire right.

In hindsight, what do you think went wrong?

In this case, as I've usually found to be the case, the candidate had the technical skills. But the key question was: Can you use those skills effectively within our environment, and will you enhance our environment along the way?

I rarely think about culture fit. Instead, I think about cultural enhancers—the people who will come in, enhance the team, and take it to the next level. They are bar raisers. They bring something that wasn't there before, and they help other team members to raise their own bars.

In this case, we actually followed a systematic process and involved the right people. But there were questions along the way. The conclusions were "We think that it will be okay." But in retrospect, thinking it would be okay was not good enough. The original hire had problems relating to people so, the second time around, the SVP spent time beyond just interviewing, in order to understand how the candidate operated in the world and whether the person was relatable to others.

What have you seen great leaders who are talent magnets do that others could learn from?

First, they don't make the recruiter the primary person on the search. They know this is their hire. The recruiter is their partner and is helping them, but the hiring manager is very actively involved. They reach out to candidates who may be hard to attract. Maybe someone is employed somewhere but you think they look really good. That person will not respond to a call from a recruiter but they may respond to you, if you say, "Hey, do you want to have some coffee? I'd love to talk with you and learn a little more about you."

Here's the other thing: They're not only actively involved in the hiring process, but they never turn it off. They're thinking about talent all the time, even when they're not filling a role. They're at an event and meet somebody. They then have that person on their radar, and will work to get to know them more, let them know more about what the company does and what it stands for.

The other thing the talent magnet does is make it clear to their direct reports that they must do the same. They cannot leave hiring to HR. We are leading this organization and we're responsible for helping to find amazing people. When it comes to talent, you can't shield yourself. You have to be out there, talking, sharing your contact information, and being accessible to people, no matter how busy you are.

What are you a broken record about?

I'm constantly harping on the fact that you're not looking for culture fit; you need diversity. You need people that work differently. Just because someone doesn't have the personality style or specific way of working in the world that you relate to most, they could be a huge cultural enhancer for your team based on what they bring. So, I help people to have a more well-rounded view of what it means to be a great fit within your organization.

Another thing with me is that the pipeline is everything. It's just like any other sales cycle: If your funnel isn't good, then you won't get down to the end of the funnel where you're going to close that candidate within the timeframe that you need to. I'm constantly assessing the funnel and pipeline.

The last thing I would say is that numbers matter. There are several different ways to measure the effectiveness of what we do. For example, many companies look at time to fill. I tend to move away from time to fill and think about quality of hire. What is the Net Promoter Score of this person once they've been with the company for three months? I want to know that both from the candidate we hired—would they join the company again?—and from the manager's perspective: would they hire this person again?

The real question is what is the quality of this hire? Are they really raising the bar in your organization? Are they helping the organization move forward in ways that you were not able to do before? Quite frankly, I believe every hire we make has the potential to do that in every job. It's not just your senior jobs; I think every person that we bring into our company has the ability to make our organization better or make it worse. So, it's a continuous process of measuring and monitoring. If those numbers are dropping for any reason, you need to know that quickly and then determine what's going wrong, what are we missing, and what needs to change to get it right. If you're not continuously measuring and adjusting, you won't meet your hiring goals.

9

Talent Makers

So, here we are.

We've covered a great deal about hiring in the last eight chapters, and we're finally ready to talk in depth about the concept behind the title of this book: Talent Makers.

Before you even picked up this book, we guess you knew that hiring was not working the way you wanted it to in your organization. You probably may have suspected that it needed to play a more important role—but how?

In these chapters we've given you a framework for measuring employee value, known as Employee Lifetime Value (ELTV). We've equipped you with a way to assess where you are in the hiring maturity curve, and we looked in depth at the four strategic competencies that must be improved to make progress along that curve.

If you put the book down now, we believe you would be armed with an entire system for being able to hire amazing talent at will. But we're not ending the book here, because to tell you the truth, having an entire system will not make any difference in your organization.

What will make the difference is when you apply that system, when *you* become the catalyst for change in your organization.

In short, when you become a Talent Maker.

In this book, we have painted a picture of what great hiring looks like, with examples from our own experience and also the many organizations we've worked with. We also have described in some detail what needs to change, from the earliest stages when a role is opened, through posting, interviewing, hiring, and onboarding. We've talked about the measurements that will tell you if you're on course, or not.

But it all is a set of potential actions—proven, effective, *potential* actions—until someone steps up and takes action.

The concept of "taking action" comes in many flavors. On one end of the spectrum you have giant, irreversible actions like jumping out of a plane. Another type of action is where you must make a series of split-second decisions the way a mountain biker does when traveling at high speed down a steep, rocky path.

Becoming great at hiring requires no skydiving-type commitments, or split-second decisions. The great news is that all the processes we've discussed can be implemented and undone, if for some reason (which we can't think of) it became necessary. You also need not make any snap judgments, but can take your time to explain, discuss, reach consensus, and implement.

Before we get into the real details about how to become a Talent Maker who is the catalyst for creating an environment of hiring excellence, let's define what the role is.

What Is a Talent Maker?

A Talent Maker is a leader who believes *and acts* as if hiring great talent is their top priority. It's a fundamental shift away from the traditional belief that talent acquisition (TA) is the role of recruiters. That's what your competition thinks. So, in order to attract great, competitive talent who can choose to work anywhere, the Talent Maker needs to put their personal efforts up front, and the force of their entire organization behind it.

We do not mean to imply that being a Talent Maker is the role of the CEO only. Ideally, the CEO is indeed onboard and they may be able to promote the fastest change. However, in our experience the catalyst for change can be any leader —of a business unit, department, or team. As we've discussed throughout this book, people generally know that the typical hiring system is broken; they just don't know how to fix it. When a breakthrough occurs on one team, before long the people in that area wonder why it took so long, and they shake their head at how it used to be done. Other groups take notice and start to ask questions: "What's this interview kit I've been hearing about?"

Let's get more specific about just what a Talent Maker is and does. You can think about a Talent Maker as having three roles for three different constituencies. You are a talent leader to your organization, a talent magnet to the talent that your company wants to hire, and a talent partner to your internal recruiting team. Each role needs some explanation.

Talent Maker as Talent Leader

A talent leader builds and leads a culture of hiring in the organization. The example they set becomes a very visible model for anyone in the organization who may wonder what it means to support a culture of hiring excellence.

All employees are tuned to receive two types of signals: what leaders say, and what they do. Employees monitor that second signal closely, because it tells them how the organization really works, despite what mission statements and press releases say.

> *Jon:* I previously worked at Johnson & Johnson. It's more than 130 years old, with 130,000 employees. They have a famous thing called their Credo, which General Johnson wrote more than a century ago.[1] The thing is, employees soon realize that they are not kidding about the Credo.
>
> First, every manager goes through Credo training: What is it? What does it mean? They discuss examples of actual decisions employees made that were affected by what the Credo says. At the company headquarters they literally have the Credo *carved in stone* in the lobby.

I have been in meetings where difficult decisions were being discussed. At one point, someone would say: "I think this is a Credo issue" and it totally changed the atmosphere in the room. People sat back: "Whoa, okay, yeah we can't mess with that" and the decision became obvious.

So, how do you promote a culture of hiring excellence as a talent leader? You can think of a leader as having three currencies: your visibility, your actions, and your time.

Your Visibility

Depending on your level in the organization, you have different opportunities to walk the talk. Consider the following:

Does anyone from recruiting get one-on-one meetings with you?

When you hold an all-hands meeting (or a smaller version of that in your area), how high on the agenda do hiring-related topics fall?

When you hold meetings with your direct reports, how often is hiring on the agenda, and how high up is it on that agenda? Is it at the end, when you're running out of time, or is it sometimes the lead-off topic?

Do you meet with every new hire early on? As we mentioned, we meet on day one with them, and also have breakfast for each hiring class.

In letters to shareholders (or to smaller constituencies as the case may be), how prominently are you talking about hiring? For example, if you're coming off a great quarter, how are you defining "great"? Is it just the standard metrics about earnings, new products, new markets, and so on? Or are you prominently ringing the bell, so to speak, when you beat your hiring goals including your diversity, equity, and inclusion (DE&I) objectives?

On the flipside, are you holding hiring managers accountable for their hiring goals? And when you fall short of your hiring objectives, how prominent is the discussion about the actions you already are implementing to correct the situation?

If you are the CEO, do you personally answer every Glassdoor rating that's left? One of the things that I (Daniel) hear about the most is how surprised people are that I monitor and respond to every comment. I also do not use some boilerplate language about "your concern has been noted," but I develop a unique response for each review. Glassdoor inserts a label of "CEO" next to each of my comments.

Here's a secret: This is an activity with a ridiculously high ROI—it literally takes a few minutes a month for me to do this, yet it separates us from at least 95 percent of companies that don't do this.

There's another mechanism at work here: All Greenhouse employees know that I reply to Glassdoor comments. Let's say we get beat up in one of those reviews. First, I reply to the reviewer; second, you can be sure that I don't want to see that type of review again, so I investigate what we could have done differently in order to ensure a better employee experience and hence a better Glassdoor outcome next time.

Your Actions

First, what high-level statements are you making about the importance of hiring? You should promote a culture where hiring goes from this standard ho-hum thing that a unit does, and you should show that it's a privilege. It needs to become a highly visible project that people vie for, because of how it's valued by the organization from the top on down. A talent leader promotes and pays off the concept that hiring—when done extremely well—is a ticket to greater things.

If someone compared the salaries of top people in your recruiting department with similar levels in other departments, what statement does the comparison make?

What are you expecting from your direct reports, in terms of being talent leaders in their own areas? Do you assume that they're as active as you are about hiring, or do you know? Do they bring up their hiring activities as often as they highlight the other key activities like product development, sales, and so on?

When someone comes to you with a *great reason* why the structured hiring process cannot be followed, what do you do? Do what you want, but in our experience there is only one answer: You need to decide in favor of the hiring process. Daniel once had that issue with a recruiter of ours working with a highly competitive candidate. She didn't have the scorecard filled out and explained that there was no time for that and other processes, that we were about to lose the candidate. Bad news: We lost the candidate in the time it took to do the process as it was designed. Good news: This shortcut maneuver never happened again. Do you think if I said, "Well okaaaaay, we'll let it go this one time ... " that it would never have happened again?

There is another, more subtle manifestation of talent leader as enforcer of process integrity. By the time candidate information reaches a senior leader, your expectation should be that the entire process has been followed. So, when you flip through the scorecards and other information, your questions aren't so much about the candidate as they are about whether the process was followed. That's because an incomplete process is no basis on which to judge a candidate.

So, in organizations on the lower region of the hiring maturity curve, the leader needs to notice things like "I know you want to give an offer to Tariq. I'm seeing in the scorecard that we interviewed intensively on 14 attributes, but why are these other two blank?"

Contrast that with what the leader will get in a company that's high on the curve, where an offer packet will contain an explanation of anticipated questions: "Here are the scorecards. By the way, you'll notice that in step two, Bill gave a thumbs-down. So, in the roundup, we asked him about that and discussed XYZ, and as a team we are comfortable with making the offer in spite of that.... "

Talent leaders must help first-time managers to get the hiring education they never got. I (Daniel) gave a lecture at the Stanford Graduate School of Business about hiring. They're a leading thinker in this area, but highly unrepresentative: Most business education is sorely lacking when it comes to hiring topics, never mind any deep treatment about hiring excellence. Most schools have very little instruction on how to hire, and if there is any focus on interviewing, it's not about how to hire, but instead about how to ace the interview and land a job. Only now are schools slowly shifting from a focus on consulting and Wall Street, to a greater focus on entrepreneurship.

In addition, many people get promoted into management without ever having gone to business school. Most first-time managers have never hired anybody before. In organizations with chaotic or inconsistent hiring practices, they learn the bad habits that we've highlighted throughout this book. It's pretty quick and easy to remember to ask the recruiter, "Where's my hire?"

Whether your managers went to business school or not, it's up to you to make up for that educational gap. You should explain that more or less their entire job hinges on how well they hire the next three people. It's a microcosm of the advice we gave the company that was on a fast track to go public; recall in Chapter 3, that we told them how billions of dollars of valuation hinged on the success of the next two or three hundred hires. It's a good use of your time to identify first-time managers, and get them started on the right path, before they need to unlearn unproductive ways.

Talent leaders need to give people the space to step back and work on the business and not just *in* it. To the untrained eye, that stepping back can look like a loss of productivity. You may hear, "Why are we talking when we should be filling roles?" or "Organizations don't make their numbers by creating more bureaucratic procedures—they make their numbers by taking action and getting people in seats."

Talent leaders need to anticipate those stated or unstated objections, and explain how building the four competencies takes time initially, but will result in a higher ELTV. They have to explain that hiring is hard work, and great hiring is not the path of least resistance in the near term. It is the path of highest benefit to the organization and its employees in the medium- and long-term.

Talent leaders sometimes need to push back hard. We've talked about the legitimate role that agencies can play, even when organizations have their own active sourcing operation. In our case one such role involved an executive search.

> *Daniel:* We were hiring an executive and I told the hiring agency that it was a priority of ours to diversify our executive team. I said my expectation was that when they sent us candidates, that it would be a diverse candidate pool.
>
> After a few weeks of looking for candidates and sending me a few, they wanted to talk: "Daniel, the truth is we're having a hard time finding diverse candidates—the talent pool is what it is." The agency person continued, "Let me ask you a question: Is this just kind of a 'check the box' thing where you want to say that you've seen a few women for this job, or what?"

I let them have it. They were trying to lead me to conclude that I was sabotaging my own efforts by trying to diversify my hire. My pushback on them was just how incredibly lazy they were being. I said, "On one level, I believe you, that if you just do the most obvious things that everyone does, you'll develop a less-diverse pool than what I'm looking for. That's not what I'm paying you all that money for. I know that it takes effort, and I know that it takes smarts to do what I'm asking you to do. My expectation is that you're going to do it."

They were using that line on the wrong guy. If I was the CEO of a furniture company and I was paying this person 100 grand to run an executive search, I'd probably figure that they know executive search the way I know sofas and loveseats. When they then say, "Look, we did the search and this is what is out there" then most CEOs would believe them.

By pushing back on the agency to really do what we needed done, they changed their approach and delivered some good candidates.

Talent leaders also need to be vocal about internal promotions. In Chapter 6, we discussed how management is often frustrated by how few employees apply for other positions. It's not uncommon for managers to feel like their employees are traitors by leaving, or another manager is poaching their talent when a move happens. It's up to the leader to make it a stated and valued goal for internal moves to occur.

When managers eventually know in their bones that an open role will be filled by great talent, then the "disloyalty" or "poaching" conclusions will melt away. Plus, they'll be on the receiving end of getting great talent from other units of the organization, without fear of offending anyone.

Your Time

If you've done even a fraction of the activities we've listed above, then hiring is likely to take a substantial fraction of your time—as it should. We caution you against anticipating that your time commitment will materially drop, the farther along you get on the maturity curve. What instead will happen is the complexion of your time will change from setting up systems, to requesting or demanding data to understand what's happened and what will happen. You'll spend time analyzing that data more deeply and demanding accountability, and these actions will change the culture of the organization. The work that great hiring requires never ends, but that's okay, given that it's firmly in the realm of one of the highest and best uses of your time.

Talent Maker as Talent Magnet

Here's the big-picture perspective on being a talent magnet:

- This person is very personally engaged in attracting and pursuing top talent—both candidates and prospects.
- They meet with prospects and help to close late-stage people.
- They help to build the organization's hiring brand by getting out there and telling the story.

Picture that you're a highly qualified and sought-after professional and you've decided to pursue some of the continuous offers and inquiries you get. You've interviewed at a few places and have rejected more than one offer. You're now down to two companies that look quite good. The recruiter calls you back from one of the two companies and says, "We're really excited about you. We can't wait for your start date. What questions do you have?" At the other company, one of the founders calls you back, and says the same thing. Are you likely to consider those to be equal calls?

Let's talk about a position that's lower in the organization by a few levels, so it's unlikely that a founder would be calling you. In the one case, you get a call with an offer from a recruiter. It's a pretty technical job, and you weren't impressed at the recruiter's grasp of the role during the interview, but it was okay. At the other company, the hiring manager was much more involved with the interview, and now the hiring manager calls you with the offer. That tells you something about the manager caring about the team because they took time out to work on building that team. They're also able to answer any questions on the spot about projects, advancement, who your core team members will be and their skills, the team culture, and so on. Which company just made the stronger case?

A talent magnet does more than close the deal with competitive candidates, though that's a big piece of it. They are also putting themselves out there, playing the long game of showing the hiring brand in an appropriate way, making connections, and cultivating relationships. Our CTO should have been deeded the table at a local watering hole in Manhattan, given how he would be there two, three, and sometimes four nights a week, talking tech.

He talked about the work we were doing, built our reputation, asked about people they knew, and connected with friends of friends. And he did it *for years*. So, when from time to time he had a role to fill, it didn't come across as a pitch, but just as today's news.

Another example involves a head of sales who attended one of the Talent Maker workshops we conducted. She told us about a blog she created about her sales team. She spent a little time each week writing posts with stories of all the cool stuff they were doing, just kind of shop talk among sales pros. Her readership steadily grew, consisting of sales professionals interested in that particular type of work. They found her commentary compelling; besides, her description of the work environment made it sound like a great place to work. In one 12-month period, she ended up making three hires from readers of her blog.

It could be that our CTO would find blog writing to be awful, and this sales pro might hate hanging out at a bar; fortunately, there are plenty of ways to be a talent magnet, so people can find the approach that works for them. Other ways to attract: being willing to speak on panels; giving interviews to magazines; participating in mentoring activities at colleges; and keeping your eyes open for awards in your area of expertise.

If you're in the C-suite, you have a megaphone. When we give a keynote to a thousand-person audience, we're always telling the story of why it's great to work here. Every time you do a thing like that, you'll hear feedback on your website or from candidates currently interviewing: "Oh, I saw your CEO at that event and she sounded really smart," or some similar comment. It's a role that only business leaders can play—not leaders from recruiting.

Talent Maker as Talent Partner

The third role of a Talent Maker is to be a partner to the recruiting team, enabling them to do their best work. It comes from realizing that the way to be successful at hiring exceptional talent is to have an exceptionally supportive business side for recruiting efforts.

There's another reason to focus so much on the recruiting process, and we've not heard it discussed anywhere else. Companies like to talk about their culture. They'll have brainstorming sessions and come up with five keywords like "resourceful" and "inclusive." Then they announce the work of the Culture Committee, print up some posters—and they end up being merely nice words on paper. A short work of fiction.

A real challenge that leaders have is how do you instill that culture in the company for real? What makes those values real is *when you use them.* And so the question is where do you get to use your values? The place where the values should be discussed daily and used as guides for decisions most often is recruiting. If you think about it, you have all these people interviewing candidates. The criteria should not just be whether they're a good programmer but whether they exhibit our values. We should hire people—or not—based on those values.

When you train interviewers to ask values-based questions, and you in fact make decisions based on those values, you're telling your whole company that these values matter. They're real, and they change how we make decisions.

Spend Time, Make Time, Show Up

When a recruiter asks you to go to an interview, regard it as a high priority. Actively participate in the interview instead of being late, or not having reviewed the Interview Kit ahead of time, or straying from the questions you're supposed to ask.

After the interview, be prompt in filling out your scorecard. Offer to call the candidate, if it's a situation where that might tip the scale for the candidate to accept an offer.

Make sure you talk about your active involvement in these processes, so as to be a model for your direct reports to follow suit.

Give Recruiters the Tools They Need to Be Successful

Most recruiters are on the back foot, so to speak. They're being asked to do too much without enough resources, which is what happens when you're regarded as a bureaucratic cost center. At the same time, it's a highly dynamic and competitive environment. The hiring environment has changed radically in less than one career's time, as we discussed. However, recruiting areas have not kept up with the times. Part of showing your commitment to great hiring is giving recruiting what it needs: Provide the right technology; staff them appropriately; pay them well; and listen to what they ask you to do.

"You're making it sound like I should just cave in and let recruiting run the show."

That would be the wrong conclusion. It's not caving in when the area most directly responsible for great hiring is fully supported. Plus remember: when recruiting does receive a higher level of support, you can reasonably hold them to a very high standard.

If you accept the role as Talent Maker, you have a big job ahead. However, you'll get no brownie points for making the job harder than it needs to be. The next chapter is about what to expect, and some navigational advice.

Note

1. https://www.jnj.com/our-heritage/timeline-of-johnson-johnson-credo-driven-decisions.

Chapter 9: Takeaways

A Talent Maker is a leader who believes *and acts* as if hiring great talent is their top priority.

It is not the role of the CEO only, but the role of any leader

Three components to being a Talent Maker are the following:

Talent Leader, who builds and leads a culture of hiring. This is the result of your visibility, your actions, and the time you spend on hiring.

Talent Magnet, who is very personally engaged in attracting and pursuing top talent. They meet with prospects and candidates, and help to close them. They also get out and support the organization's hiring brand.

Talent Partner is a true supporter of the recruiting team, enabling them to do their best work. They make time to work closely with recruiters, they make interviews and scorecards a priority, and they give recruiters the resources they need.

Expert Insights: Maia Josebachvili

Maia Josebachvili has had a long career around great winning teams. She's worked at a number of companies, started her own company, joined Greenhouse and was instrumental there, and was Head of People at Stripe.

What is it that a great leader does that others don't do?

I've been fortunate in my career to work with some exceptional leaders. Though their working styles vary, there is a common thread I've observed in all—they have the consummate "tell me how I can help" attitude.

We had a great new leader join the company and in his first week he emailed me and our head of recruiting and asked simply, "What can I do?" He attended our recruiting all hands in his first month, introduced himself, and said, "I'm here to help. We're going to build this amazing team together."

Another woman came in and right off the bat wanted to know the history of the recruiting process. "What's a sacred cow that I should be aware of? Where's the room to innovate?" She clearly wanted to partner with us on the recruiting process and build the best team together.

Those are just two examples out of many. I've found that the best leaders see themselves and recruiting as true partners.

Let's say you've been in recruiting a long time but you're new to your company and the leader is not fully onboard with these concepts of great hiring. How do you effect change upward to the leader?

Evidence-based approaches often work best in these cases. If you look at the strongest teams in an organization—the ones that consistently out-perform expectations and navigate a changing landscape—they often have a strong hiring culture in common. This kind of culture is set from the top, with a leader that prioritizes great hiring. As an example, I worked with a great C-level exec who described hiring as always one of his top three priorities. Though he had a team of 100-plus, he was always available to help. He'd say, "Whether you're hiring a director or an entry-level role, if I can help get on a call and close the candidate, I'll do it." And he always did. Not surprisingly, he had one of the strongest teams in the company. So, if you have a leader who isn't quite on board yet, I'd suggest finding examples of what "great" looks like and showing them the difference that a strong hiring culture can make on the overall performance of the team.

Let's say you come into a company and there is an inconsistent level of hiring maturity. What would be the first thing you put into place to get them higher on the curve?

It's important to start with the CEO. It all flows from there. If hiring is not a regular topic at leadership team meetings, it's hard to picture how the whole organization will evolve their hiring maturity. Getting higher on the curve often requires some cultural evolution: You're evolving your articulation of what is most important and where people should be spending their time.

One tactical and visible manifestation of this is the company all-hands meeting. I'd want to make sure the CEO and senior leadership team are talking about how we're doing with hiring: celebrating successes, reinforcing behaviors, and sharing areas of concern that they'd like to see improve. This could take a few forms—for example, talking about the new hires that we're very excited about and giving a little summary of the work it took to find them. I've found it inspiring to hear from leaders that they didn't want to settle and kept interviewing, even after the 50th one, because finding the right fit was that critical.

It's also important to insist on accountability at the leadership and management level. Recruiting and People teams are here to *enable* great hiring, but ultimately it's on each manager and leader to ensure they're improving their hiring maturity and building the best team. One great way to do this is to include a hiring goal in each team's goals at the time they are set. Then, just like you would review sales performance at the end of the quarter, you also look at how the team did against their overall hiring target and key roles for the quarter.

What are your tips for instilling a strong People culture on your teams?

Be explicit about the importance of hiring and people, and then reinforce that consistently through your behaviors, what you recognize, and where you spend your time.

Early on, I was running an area and my manager asked me, "Who are the rising stars on your team who should be on my radar?" I thought that was a great question, and I started to ask it of my direct reports. Then every other month or so, I'd hold a casual coffee roundtable with the folks who were identified. I was explicit in its purpose: "I've heard you've been having a ton of impact. First, thank you! I wanted to make sure you knew that I and your manager saw that. And second, I want to hear from you. You have a great perspective into the org that I don't have and I'd love your advice about what else we should be doing." These meetings were some of my favorites and I always walked away more energized and with better insight into how we could continue to improve our function.

This example is more about demonstrating the importance of people once they're on your team, but the same goes for hiring. I make it a point to publicly recognize leaders for making great hires and make sure the team knows how critical I think it is for our ability to have an impact.

Can you talk a little bit about leaders you've worked with who themselves were great at working with candidates or getting personally involved in the hiring process on their teams?

One key practice they have is in communicating personally with candidates. We all know that the best candidates are inundated with in-mails, and recruiter emails can easily slip through the cracks. If a recruiter is having a hard time getting a top-tier candidate on the phone, I've found that an email from the leader directly can often tip that candidate over the edge.

It's a similar dynamic when it comes to landing competitive candidates. The best people often have multiple competing offers, and a company's closing approach can be the decision-maker. A call with a senior leader who is a couple of rungs up the reporting chain can go a long way to making a candidate feel valued and excited about the opportunity.

You have an unusual perspective on reference checks. Could you please describe it?

This is an underutilized but critical part of the interview process. Let me put it this way: if I had to pick between doing interviews or checking references when hiring and I could only do one, I'd lean towards doing the references. This is especially true for senior leaders who are usually strong in the skill of interviewing. I also think leaders are better positioned than recruiters to get the most out of those reference checks. This is not a knock on the recruiters—there's just a different conversation that two CMOs will have, and the long-term relationship and reputation is too valuable for them to not be honest.

If I'm the leader doing the reference check, I first do a bunch of warm-up questions. Then I basically hinge most of it on my last question, which is "Where would you rate this person out of everyone you've ever worked with? Top 50 percent? Top 20 percent?" I never go much higher than the top 15 percent because I don't want to lead them. But if they're not replying with a number around the top five percent, I have pause. Every reference can share strengths and areas of development, but that doesn't give very clear insight into whether they're one of the best. Another question I like is "Let's fast-forward—pretend that I hire this person and it doesn't work out. What's your prediction as to why you think it didn't work out?"

10

Changing Minds

Throughout this book we've discussed the common but sad state of hiring in most organizations—and how it does not have to be that way. We've shown you a method for making hiring a valued, core function of your organization, and how you as the Talent Maker can be a catalyst for that transformation.

Even so, we have no delusions about that transformational journey. We know how hard change can be, especially when the ultimate goal of that change is no form of easy street. Even in the best-run organizations with amazing hiring systems, it's still a lot of hard work to make it work. The only consolation prize for all that hard work is to be able to hire great talent at will. We think that's a pretty good prize, after all.

Therefore, we want to give you some techniques and observations that we've found to be helpful when you endeavor to move an organization along the path of change. Please note that there are plenty of textbooks written about change management, and some companies have entire units devoted to program management; this chapter does not pretend to be even an introduction to that large topic. Instead, we want to describe some of the specific challenges you'll encounter, and some of the ways we and other organizations have dealt with them.

Unconscious Pressure

Jon: A friend of mine was telling me about an interesting conversation he had with his wife. They live not far from a Whole Foods market, and also a standard-type supermarket. One day, he noticed something interesting: When his wife went to Whole Foods Market, she brought canvas bags for the groceries, but on days that she went to the supermarket, she brought home their plastic bags. He asked her about that. "Well, it's good for the environment when I use canvas bags at Whole Foods." He said, "I get that—but why then don't you bring those bags along to the supermarket?"

They got into what was happening there, and it turned out that if you bring your own plastic bags to Whole Foods, people glare at you. There is social pressure. But at the local supermarket, people could not care less what sort of bags you bring. Of course, there's also the structural cue that Whole Foods doesn't even offer plastic bags, and the supermarket has them ready to go, with the canvas bags off to the side.

This is all to say that even without any courses and certifications, large numbers of people can change their ways, without necessarily realizing what's happening. It takes time and intentional design, but it works. We've described how organizations reach a tipping point where it becomes more painful to neglect to fill out a scorecard or prepare for a roundup—and incur the wrath of your peers—instead of just doing the work.

Recruiting Operations

Because we're writing this book for leaders and many of them are on the business side, we don't want to assume that you know the various roles that recruiting areas typically have. Earlier, we mentioned how vital the recruiting ops role is to organizations, so let's look at why this role is so important, and why it merits your attention, even if you're on the business side.

The job of the recruiter is to find candidates and guide them through the process, which they're in charge of. They are assisted by a coordinator, who does all the interview scheduling. They typically meet candidates at the front door and escort them around the building. Then there are specialist roles like sourcers, who spend all day researching potential candidates and emailing them. If the department is large enough, there will be a recruiting leader.

Any way you look at it, recruiting is a really busy job. There are so many moving parts and you're juggling many candidates at one time, trying to make sure that everyone is followed up with, internal folks are doing what they're supposed to do, and so on. If recruiters want to have any hope of moving the organization up the maturity curve, they need to step back and think about processes, tools, and data. The problem is that the skills that make for a great recruiter are different from the skills necessary to be great at logistics and processes. At some point, the head of recruiting—if that person is smart and wants to remain sane—will turn to a right-hand person who may be a coordinator and say, "Hey, are you good at spreadsheets? You are? Cool. I have a task for you."

First the job is just about making an inventory of all the tools, spreadsheets, forms, and procedures that happen in recruiting. Pretty soon, it becomes obvious that a lot of manual, unnecessary work is being done to reenter information between tools, chase people for information, remember to do certain things at certain times, and so on.

If this "spreadsheet person" is any good, things start to get automated. It might start with just spreadsheets being linked. The spreadsheet person will also start to produce reports that provide new insights into what's going on in recruiting.

In an organization that's attempting to move up the curve, this person gradually becomes more central to the smooth functioning of the department. They're doing the key function of recruiting ops, whether they call it that or not.

At some point the role evolves to be full-time. By this point, the people who are in favor of the new, more systematized approach begin to realize something: The person doing recruiting ops should not be this junior coordinator who's good at spreadsheets; it should actually be a senior person.

One of the growing pains on this path is there may be something of a power struggle at this point. This role that started in recruiting has morphed into a power center of its own—as it should, in our opinion. Operations starts to tell recruiting that certain systems need to be followed. Ops controls all the systems, all the data, processes, and training, so how everybody works in the hiring process flows through the hands of Ops. At one point recruiters push back, saying, "Hey, we're the people who go find candidates, okay? We're the ones making the hires. You should be making our lives better, not more rigid."

Ops says, "No, actually I'm taking control over this process that previously was not a process at all but a mess. We're going to agree on a centralized process, and centralized stages, data, and vendor management. We all have to do the hiring process the same way. In fact, here's the deal: The way we're going to judge your success is based on what happens in the system. If you work outside the system, you won't get credit for that work."

Obviously, this is an inflection point or crossroads for the organization. If senior leadership supports Ops, then systematic processes become the way hiring is done. That's the definition of Stage 3 of the hiring maturity curve. But if the power struggle resolves in favor of someone who argues against these systems—perhaps equating them with a bureaucracy—that would be a setback for structured hiring.

You, as a Talent Maker, should throw your weight behind the Ops position. Of course, if you have an Ops person who is not diplomatic and takes on a certain Napoleon complex, that's not good. Ops needs to be part of the team and must persuade more than dictate. But this person needs support in order to get to the point where all the pain of doing things differently begins to pay off in smoother processes and better hires.

"That all sounds like what we want to do, but we can't afford a senior Recruiting Ops position at the moment."

That's fine. In our experience, organizations don't create full-time recruiting ops positions until they have around 700 to 1,000 employees. If you are under that size, it's fine to have someone who fills the role on less than a full-time basis. What's crucial is not whether the position is part- or full-time; instead, it's whether the difficult work of systematizing the hiring process is being supported and enforced— or not.

Catalyst Events

The Recruiting Ops position is about creating a unit that helps to drive change. But there are other circumstances that accelerate or force change.

A new hire. Sometimes a new head of recruiting comes in because the previous one was failing. The new person has a mandate to make things better. They may already have experienced a great culture of hiring at their previous post. In that case, one of their first moves in the new organization may be to upgrade systems and put in place a structured hiring approach. They come in and say, "Here are the reports I want to see every quarter." They hit the ground running and people quickly realize that a new sheriff is in town.

Cash infusion. Startups pursue venture capital (VC) funding and when they get it, it's like the dog running after the car and catching it. Now what? The clock is immediately ticking to show results, and they need to hire hundreds of people, fast. If this company has been advised by an incubator or by someone with sufficient scars, then it may realize it needs a structured approach to hiring. The next couple of hundred hires—if done right—could mean literally billions of dollars of valuation.

DE&I issues. It may have come to the attention of employees via surveys that the organization is woefully behind on making progress toward its DE&I goals, or even having any. The old argument of "it's a top-of-funnel problem" may have worked for a quarter or two, but now the board is demanding progress.

Reading this book. For an organization, meaningful change may be a hard, lengthy process. But the catalyst or spark to get it going can come from many sources—including you. We suggest that you put time on your side and begin (or accelerate) the Structured Hiring process before external, urgent circumstances force it. There is never a good time to be bad at hiring, but now is a great time to get better at it.

Finding a Foothold

We often get a question 'along the lines of "So if we want to start some-where, just to get moving, where should that be?" We have two answers, relating to "who" and "what."

Identify an Ally

We strongly suggest that when starting the structured hiring journey—or when embarking on a new, big piece of it—that you not try to pull it off for the whole organization at once. If you're in recruiting, find a friendly hiring manager who seems to be open-minded and also influential. In effect, you're beta testing your rollout and can gather valuable feedback about the questions they asked you and the sequence of steps you took. Now you can incorporate that knowledge when working with the next unit.

If you're a business leader, then work to get aligned with a recruiter in order to try this new way together, to set an example for the rest of the organization. Either way, there's nothing like some social proof from peers to get the ball rolling. After a hiring cycle or two, someone will have hired an all-star and will be talking with the head of engineering: "Why are you doing it the old way? You're crazy. This is great; there's no way I'm going back." That may be all that's needed to get another group on board.

Identify an Entry Point

One great place to begin this process is with the interview kit. First, it doesn't require a lot of training and buy-in. People were going to spend time interviewing anyway, so this is not asking for any more time. On the contrary: In the past I might have sent you a résumé with no guidance about the interview. Now, I'll send you a link to the résumé and the scorecard, which will make your life easier because you have a script for the interview. That will have been done by the hiring manager ally.

A better interview kit then makes it more likely to have a better roundup. People are looking at the agreed-upon scorecard and that will help to give structure to the discussion. There still may be groupthink where the loudest or most senior person influences the discussion. But at least if the scorecards are completed in advance, there is less chance for the same level of domination to occur.

After you do a better roundup like this, then you can ask, "How does everyone feel about the process we just followed, versus how we used to do it?" People are likely to say, "Yeah that was good but I think we should change this one question ... " in which case you're off to the races.

Another entry point, as we mentioned in the last chapter, is approvals. The idea of approvals as change management is powerful. People often think of approvals as a budget function, and that certainly is important. But if you're the department head and you have the ability to approve or not approve any opening for a new job in your department, that gives you the opportunity to do some quality control.

You can say, "Okay, we're opening this job. Have you discussed as a team what the criteria should be? If so, show me the scorecard." If they haven't shown you a scorecard, you ask them to follow the process and create one. Pretty soon, it becomes obvious that the only way that job is going to be posted on the website is if the process is followed.

"But what if our CEO is the problem? What if that person doesn't see the value of this whole system?"

It happens. The best thing is not to try to persuade them directly, but do what we suggested above: find a hiring manager with the right mindset and influence, and create a success story. That's a win-win because the hiring manager becomes the successful pioneer, you get your case study and a happy ambassador, and the CEO can see the results.

Slow Is Fast

If someone looked at the first few moments of an airplane taking off, and projected that as an indicator of success, it would not look good. Here we have all engines roaring at full blast, and at first we're crawling! Then we pick up some speed, but still are on the ground. Plus, the end of the runway is coming up fast. This certainly does not look like it's going to work.

There are also some negative indicators when starting down the path of structured hiring.

It feels like a lot of upfront work. In the old world, if you wanted a job posted, great; someone copies and pastes a job description from the Internet and slaps it up. You get some candidates by this afternoon. In the new world, we first get six people together. The hiring manager and others think hard about the criteria for the job and write some questions. It may take a few days to make sure that the questions are correct and we've thought through how all the interviews will fit together.

Once that work is done, you can indeed move quickly. And once you get a candidate that you like, you can move really fast to make an offer—faster than typically happened in the old world. You'll be quicker in all the right ways, but it definitely feels slower up front.

Good Data Takes Time

Sometimes the catalyst event for a CEO is lack of data. They realize that they're not making their hires, and they want to get to the bottom of it. So, they get an Applicant Tracking System (ATS) like Greenhouse or any other one—and they still are frustrated. The truth is there is no data because the organization has been living outside their tools, and running their own menagerie of systems that don't talk to each other. Migrating garbage data to a new system only means you have a new system with garbage data.

You have to use structured hiring for a while, and be disciplined about how you create data. Pretty soon, you'll have a little bit of pipeline data you can trust, and that amount will steadily grow. After a couple of rounds of hires, you'll have enough data to begin to learn something. It's a hard reality that even though you've switched over to the structured world, you won't realize all of your data dreams immediately.

Two Problems to Avoid

You may find it surprising for us to say this: Buying Greenhouse is not the solution. Don't get us wrong—we think it's a great product. But if you buy the product, plug it in, and continue in your chaotic ways, you'll scratch your head and wonder what all the "structured hiring" fuss was all about, because you won't see any particular benefit.

You'd be better off taking what you've learned in this book and implementing it using spreadsheets and documents, rather than buying Greenhouse and not working on the four competencies we've discussed.

The second problem to avoid is buying any good ATS and assigning its implementation to the wrong person. We can recall a situation where a company bought our product and asked the office manager/receptionist to implement it. He was likely working a full-time role of vendor management, employee support, and greeting guests at the front desk, but nothing relating to hiring. It was clear that someone had told him, "Hey, here's this Greenhouse thing we got. Maybe you can find some time to use it and help us with recruiting."

The investment you will make in your next 10 hires will have a significant effect on the future of your company. Why should the person running the system be any less strategic than the person running your sales organization? You would never put your office manager in charge of your sales organization.

"A" players hire "A" players; "B" players hire "C" players. Consider giving the task to the most badass person in your company, because what if they hired 10 more badass people? What more impactful thing could you do? Besides, the optics of who is involved in structured hiring will telegraph to the organization a strong message about the real value and priority of the effort.

Being Great Does Not Mean Being Perfect

Let's say you take to heart what we've discussed in this book and you start the structured hiring journey. You become a Talent Maker and begin with a core of like-minded people, and you work on the four competencies. Over time, you move from a chaotic environment, through the inconsistent phase to consistent and then finally to strategic.

If you do all that, there is zero doubt that you will have any difficulty hiring amazing talent. But nothing is perfect. This is not a roadmap to a fantasyland where all is serene and perfect. So, what are the challenges and realities that organizations face, even when they're world-class at hiring? We can think of four.

1. **Humans operate the system.** These biological organisms are pretty amazing, but they also have good days and bad days. In sufficient numbers, someone is always doing great work and someone else is messing up. Sometimes, that occurs in an interview in the form of a stupid remark; other times, it's biases bubbling up in decision-making. Fortunately, a structured approach helps to limit—but not eliminate—the dumb stuff.

2. **Hiring is intensely competitive and dynamic.** Even if you're great at hiring, guess what—the other team has varsity jackets, too. You will face stiff competition for top talent. Occasionally, you will get out-recruited for a candidate. A lot of companies want great talent as much as you do, and some of them have a lot more money than you do, not to mention unlimited sushi bars, dry cleaning, stock options—the list goes on.

   Hiring is also dynamic. As we discussed, what once was a great way to reach certain types of talent can quickly get nuked by recruiter spam and it stops being a place where talent congregates. One door closes and another opens. It's your job to find the next door.

3. **Hiring is probabilistic.** There is an element of chance, no matter how carefully we run the process. You methodically develop rating criteria and sift and sort the applicants. You then effectively interview them and make them run the gauntlet. Even so, you've spent how much time with them? Two hours? Five hours? And you're going to hire them to work 2,000 hours a year for several years, interacting with who-knows-what situations down the road.

   Our suggestions will reduce bias and bring more reliable data to a previously haphazard decision. But it's important to remember that humans are involved, so it won't be perfect data, and there will still be some personal biases. If you have a lousy approach to hiring and you hire 50 sales development reps (SDRs) next year, a bunch will be average, 14 might be terrible, and maybe 6 are great. If you implement structured hiring, you will not drop the terrible hires to zero. But you may only have 10 bad hires and you may boost the great hires from 6 to 10. That may not sound like much, but if you trade 4 terrible hires for 4 great hires, that could be the difference between missing or making your year.

4. **Hiring is one of several priorities.** As much as we are dedicated to the idea that hiring is critically important, every company—ours included—must balance the time and attention given to hiring against the other critical functions like product development, marketing, sales, and so on. Our goal is that hiring is practiced with as much rigor and discipline as any of those other processes, because the quality of talent directly and materially affects the overall success of the company.

Chapter 10: Takeaways

The Talent Maker is a catalyst for transforming an organization into a place where hiring excellence is a top priority. That involves a continuous focus on leading and supporting people along that journey.

A major force for supporting that change is Recruiting Operations. You need a department, or person, or part of a person (depending on your size) who controls all the systems, data, processes, and training.

Identify an ally. Don't try to change an organization all at once. Instead, find a friendly hiring manager or other well-respected, influential ally, and start the transformation there.

Identify an entry point. When looking for what aspect of structured hiring to start with, consider creating a better interview kit, which can pay dividends the first time it's used. Also think about focusing on approvals as a leverage point to influence change.

Good data takes time. You need to run a structured-hiring process for a cycle or two in order to begin to see useful data, so patience is required.

Great hiring is hard, but it's absolutely worth it. When you invest the time and energy into being able to hire great talent at will, you'll have harnessed the most powerful of all sustainable competitive advantages.

11

Final Thoughts

Great hiring—if done well—is not easy. That's not the promise we make. Great hiring is difficult, and so is software engineering, accounting, sales, and being an excellent executive. It's competitive, dynamic, and just plain hard. But when you're great at hiring, you feel justifiably confident and everyone can see the results. When you're bad at hiring, the effects ripple throughout the company.

As the nature of work has shifted and great talent has more power than ever, hiring has emerged as a reason why some organizations enjoy outsized success. Most organizations haven't figured out how to adapt their hiring approach, and that means the ability to hire great talent at will is very much a competitive advantage.

When is the right time to put into place structured hiring?

It's natural to wonder if the involved techniques we've covered are maybe overkill for very small organizations. In the early Greenhouse days, we attended a conference with a whole bunch of different startup entrepreneurs. Somebody asked, "At what stage of your company should you start to really focus on culture and people practices?" When they asked this of first-time founders, the answer was maybe 50 to 100 employees. When they asked the same question of

237

second- and third-time founders, the answer was *day one*. They had lived through the pain of doing it wrong, and once was enough. You're never too small to be putting these practices in place, even if they're done semi-manually on spreadsheets and documents.

When do you step back and work on the business?

We've discussed at some length how it's absolutely vital for you to find the time—your personal time and that of the people who report to you—to work on the business and not just in it, hamster-wheel style.

We mentioned above how founders who have been around the block know to work on better hiring systems from day one. We also talk regularly with recruiters who started in small organizations, grew quickly, sometimes failed miserably, and soon were themselves looking for a job. In their case, what they learned to do on day one at their next job is to get hiring right from the start.

We have been privileged to get to help thousands of organizations to embrace the hiring challenge, work their way up the maturity curve, and succeed in attracting the talent they need for the environments they face. We hope the lessons in this book will serve as a catalyst for your own organization.

Acknowledgments

Since 2012, we've been fortunate to get to build and lead this company, playing a part in the journey of thousands of companies and how they are reckoning with hiring today. This book is an encapsulation of all that we've learned in this time from our unique vantage point.

So, we'd like to start our acknowledgments by thanking all of the organizations, recruiters, and Talent Makers who have allowed us to watch and learn from them. Your intense usage of our product (and never-ending feature requests) point the way for us to where the world is going.

As we came up to speed in the HR tech world, a few of the old (old!) hands have been critical in providing us with context and laughing when we thought we'd come up with some brilliant idea that it turns out had been done 20 years before. Big shout-out to Katrina Kibben, George LaRocque, Tim Sackett, John Sumser, William Tincup, and Stacy Zapar.

We've been blessed with a number of advisors and mentors, all of whom predate Greenhouse but continue to help to this day. Thank you to Tina Sharkey, Jason Lemkin, Matt Glickman, Mark Selcow, Luke Flemmer, and Maia Josebachvili.

Thanks to our investors and board members who believed us when they didn't have to and gave us a chance at building this company. Thank you to Bill Lohse, Mike Hirshland, Mamoon Hamid, Matt Cohler, Nabil Mallick, Francisco Alvarez-Demalde, and Astha Malick.

Between the two of us, we know how to do a handful of things. But writing and publishing a book isn't one of them! So, huge thanks to Carin Van Vuuren for being the driving force in making this happen, Jonathan Rozek for molding our fuzzy, rambling ideas into coherent, lively text, Mike Campbell at Wiley for his guidance, and all the Greenhouse team members who brought this over the finish line.

And, of course, thanks to the following people for participating in interviews: Gerry Alvarez, Tope Awotona, Porter Braswell, Katie Burke, Joelle Emerson, Jan Fiegel, Shauna Geraghty, Maia Josebachvili, Jill Macri, Pattie Money, Beth Steinberg, Andres Traslavina, Arthur Yamamoto, and Daniel Yanisse.

The best proof point for the ideas in this book is the group of employees we've hired at Greenhouse. Thank you to all the Greenies who have entrusted us with their careers and make Greenhouse what it is.

And finally, we'd like to thank our families for contributing their time, money, support, and *endless* patience. It is no small burden to support entrepreneurs starting a company that probably won't work, and we thank you for indulging us.

Thanks most of all to our amazing wives (the real brains behind the operation), Alison and Megan. The first moment we had belief in Greenhouse was when Alison rendered her judgment: "You know, that's not a *terrible* idea." And the key unlock to our working relationship in the early days was when Megan sat Jon down and explained how to work effectively with Daniel: "He thinks by talking, so you should just ignore most of what he says."

And the rest is history.

About the Authors

Daniel Chait and Jon Stross co-founded Greenhouse in 2012. Greenhouse is the hiring software company that helps businesses become great at hiring through a powerful approach, complete suite of software and services, and large partner ecosystem—so businesses can hire for what's next.

Daniel Chait, CEO and Co-founder, Greenhouse

Daniel has been an entrepreneur most of his career. Prior to Greenhouse, he co-founded Lab49, a global firm providing technology consulting solutions for the world's leading investment banks. Through Daniel's firsthand experience as an entrepreneur, he has seen how valuable hiring and talent are to building world class teams.

A proud graduate of the University of Michigan, Daniel has a Bachelor of Science in Engineering degree in computer engineering (#GoBlue!).

Outside of work, Daniel's personal interests include camping and the outdoors, cooking, and most of all, being a dad. Daniel lives in the Northeast with his wife and son, where they balance being a two-CEO household.

Jon Stross, President and Co-founder, Greenhouse

Jon drives the vision and strategy of the Greenhouse product, and works closely with customers in their journey to move up the Hiring Maturity Curve.

Jon's roots in product go back more than 20 years. At BabyCenter, he led and championed what became the leading site for new and expecting parents. (Jon admits that at the time he had never even changed a baby's diaper before!) As General Manager of International at BabyCenter, now a Johnson & Johnson company, Jon steered its growth from a US business with a small UK site, to a global business reaching tens of millions of unique visitors per month. Jon was also a member of the founding team at Merced Systems, an enterprise performance management software company.

Jon, like Daniel, graduated from the University of Michigan, with a degree in political science (unlike Daniel). Jon lives in New York with his wife and daughter. In his free time, you can find him doing whatever his daughter tells him to do.

Index